LAKEVIEW CEMETERY

of

BURLINGTON, VERMONT

LAKEVIEW CEMETERY

of

BURLINGTON, VERMONT

THEA LEWIS

THE
History
PRESS

Published by The History Press
Charleston, SC
www.historypress.com

Copyright © 2020 by Thea Lewis

All rights reserved

First published 2020

Manufactured in the United States

ISBN 9781467142809

Library of Congress Control Number: 2020930491

CONTENTS

Contents

ACKNOWLEDGEMENTS

Many thanks to The History Press and Arcadia Publishing for their continued interest in my work and to my editors, Mike Kinsella and Ashley Hill, who helped guide my way. Thanks are also due to my husband, Roger Lewis, who keeps the home fires burning while I write, and, last but not least, to Burlington Cemetery assistant Holli Bushnell, whom I have dubbed the queen of Lakeview Cemetery. She not only knows where the bodies are buried, she knows how they lived before they got there.

INTRODUCTION

Lakeview Cemetery is one of the sites I recommend visiting to out-of-town guests who take my Queen City Ghostwalk haunted history tours. It's just one of the jewels in Burlington's crown, but in many ways, it's the most magnificent. Situated on the north end of the town that gave birth to Ben & Jerry's Ice Cream, Lakeview Cemetery is a gracious respite from the hustle and bustle of city living. The Victorian lawn park cemetery, one of many that were designed across the country after the Civil War, was first opened to the public in 1872 and was entered into the National Register of Historic Places in 1999.

Beautiful year round, but particularly so from late May to late September, Lakeview's winding paths are one of the best ways to get to know the city of Burlington. Early risers can take advantage of this wonderful glimpse into Burlington's past at times when the cemetery is most peaceful. There's nothing like a sun-dappled, history filled stroll through Lakeview with a morning cup of joe, looking at the monuments and written tributes that were created for people who gave Burlington's streets their names and helped shape the place that's been called one of America's "Most Livable Cities." Adsit, Flynn, Howard, Mayo, Stannard, Wells, Woodbury and the rest of the characters inside this book were Burlington citizens who put their stamp on the city, the nation and, in some cases, the world. Lakeview Cemetery has been filled with fascinating people whose contributions are too numerous to cover in the pages of just one book.

The burial ground of Lakeview Cemetery was designed by Vermont architect E.C. Ryder, whose other notable works include the Kilburn and Gates Mill on Kilburn Street and Church Street's Bacon Block (both in Burlington) and the Franklin County Courthouse in Saint Albans, Vermont. Ryer also designed the Sexton's house, which is to the right of the cemetery as you pass through the gates. A receiving vault, which is located within the cemetery, to the left of the stairs and across from the cemetery gate, was added a year later. In 1874, John Purple Howard donated a large fountain, which cost around $1,200, and later that same year, he donated the money that was needed to purchase the cemetery's main entrance pillars and iron gates. More fountains were soon added, along with a hothouse, where flowers were cultivated to decorate the grounds, and, ultimately, the Louisa Howard Chapel.

Burlington's "new" cemetery was a place where members of the community could gather to throw a picnic, spreading quilts beside friends and neighbors to share gossip from the week gone by and make plans for the week ahead. Some families, who planned their future interments at Lakeview,

The Lakeview fountain. *Photograph courtesy of Thea Lewis.*

had departed loved ones dug up from other burial grounds around the city and re-buried there. If you died in Burlington in the late 1800s, Lakeview was the place to be.

Burlington's cemeteries fall under the umbrella of the city's parks department, and the department's staff does a wonderful job of maintaining the grounds—so much of the location's grace and grandeur remains. I love Lakeview in the morning, but it's a perfect place for a stroll at any time of day. (Sans pooch, please. No dogs allowed.) Most of the time, you'll only hear the rustling of leaves from a wonderful variety of trees—including eastern hemlock and Norway spruce, yellow birch and Kentucky coffeetree, just to name a few—at the cemetery. While strolling the grounds, one can almost hear the murmured conversations of visitors from long ago. There, visitors will find monuments from the 1800s and some that are much more recent. Visitors should take a moment to ponder the origins of the stones that have either been weathered into anonymity by the elements or fallen into disrepair, without descendants to care for them.

From the Louisa Howard Chapel to the cemetery's breathtaking overlook, Lakeview Cemetery in Burlington is chock-full of history, from a handful of wars and some of the state's most interesting periods of industry and change. There, visitors will find stones inscribed with the names of magnates and mayors, philosophers and philanthropists. Inventors and innovators are buried there but so are the humble, the helpless, and even the unknown. Some of the cemetery's monuments belong to citizens who are not yet dead, and each is interesting in its own way.

The following is a look inside the lives, deaths, customs and behaviors of Burlington's citizens who have been interred in one of Vermont's most beautiful final resting places, Lakeview Cemetery, through the years—from 1872 to the present day.

1.

AN ORGANIZED AFTERLIFE

The word "cemetery" comes from a combination of Greek and Latin words that translate to mean, "Sleeping place." Through the much of the nineteenth century, people died at home, and visitations—where people had the opportunity to pay their last respects—also usually happened at home, in the parlor (or the space that we'd call the living room today), if you were lucky enough to have one of those. After a proper period of pre-burial mourning, the deceased, no matter their station in life, were removed from their homes and taken to their place of "eternal sleep," which was often a churchyard or a plot of family land. But not everyone had family land, and churchyards got mighty crowded once cities became industrialized. So, burial plots were moved, usually to the edge of town, behind a fence and a tall gate. This lessened people's fears of congested burial grounds becoming public health hazards, spreading diseases like cholera, and it made the public feel more secure about its food and water supplies. This also kept the public from having to think about the dead all the time—while a cemetery is a nice place to visit, people don't want to live there. (People were also probably comforted by the fact that they had a much better chance of surviving a zombie uprising if the dead are in fenced and gated "communities.")

Seriously, though, America's custom of interring the dead in large, common, burial grounds began with the creation of Mount Auburn Cemetery in Cambridge, Massachusetts, on land that had originally been named Stone's Farm. Locals called it as "Sweet Auburn" in reference to a poem by Oliver Goldsmith titled, "The Deserted Village." The idea for

Mount Auburn was conceived in 1925 by a doctor named Jacob Bigelow, who was concerned about the health ramifications of burying the dead under churches and the lack of space in these burial grounds. Mount Auburn was designed by Henry Alexander Scammell Dearborn, the first president of the Massachusetts Horticultural Society, along with Dr. Bigelow and landscape designer Alexander Wadsworth. An unofficial guide to the grounds titled, *Picturesque Pocket Companion and Visitor's Guide Through Mt. Auburn*, was available when the grounds were dedicated in 1831. In the guide are descriptions of notable monuments and a collection of writings —both poetry and prose—on the subject of death, by well-known writers, including Nathaniel Hawthorne and Willis Gaylord Clark.

In his 2011 book, *Cemeteries*, author Keith Eggener had a lot to say about the evolution of the American graveyard. In an interview with the *Atlantic*, he explained that, as a kid, he always liked cemeteries, because they were "kind of like parks without the crowd." The first lawn park cemeteries, often planned by architects, were all designed with intentional grids, winding paths, ornamental plantings and pretty views. Eggener explained, "Cemeteries operate as alternate cities, cities of the dead. They are often

The city vault. *Photograph courtesy of Thea Lewis.*

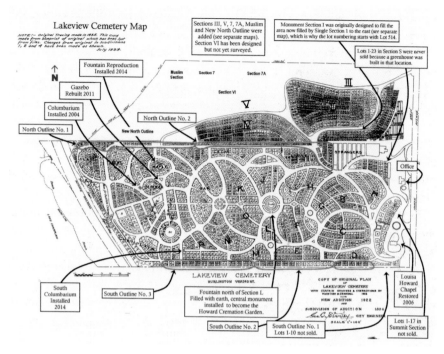

A map of Lakeview Cemetery. *Photograph courtesy of the City of Burlington, Vermont.*

very complexd." Even a cemetery's elaborate entrance gate is a symbol that visitors are entering one world, while leaving another behind. Like the world of the living, a cemetery's landscape is ever-changing. The change is gradual, sure, but stones are added, plants grow and other developments adjacent to graveyards affect their landscapes.

Styles change, too; it's particularly interesting to wander through Lakeview, and other cemeteries, to see the differences in the styles of the monuments from generation to generation. Early tombstones can seem humble, even utilitarian, while tombstones from the mid-1800s started to develop more individuality, with images and hidden meanings that were used to evoke proud and tender emotions—wheat symbolized a long life, and a carved hand with the index finger pointing upward symbolized the hope of heaven. The symbolism of birds dates back to ancient Egypt, and, depending on a bird's design, it can represent a child or a soul's flight to heaven. Figures of dogs can imply loyalty or that the master entombed there was worth loving. An anchor, often found on sailors' stones, is a symbol of hope and steadfastness; early Christians used it as a way to disguise an image

Iconic imagery of children's graves. *Photograph courtesy of Thea Lewis.*

of the cross. Then, there are the other heart wrenching symbols: little lambs, puppies and tiny, empty baby shoes.

In the mid-twentieth century, stones started to become more streamlined again, a sign of the times. The Space Age favored buildings with clean lines, and the monuments of the time followed suit. But with new engraving technologies, recent stones have, again, become embellished, ushering in a new era, in which the realistic likenesses of the deceased look back at us from glossy marble or granite surfaces.

2

LOUISA HOWARD

A SELFLESS BENEFACTRESS

A lovingly restored chapel sits at the Southeast corner of Lakeview Cemetery, just inside the main gate at 455 North Avenue. It would likely not exist without its namesake, who gifted it to the City in 1882.

Local philanthropist Louisa Howard, sister of the likeminded John Purple Howard was, inarguably, one of the most selfless women Burlington has seen. Even as she was dying, she asked that money not be wasted on fancy memorial tributes her life but given to those less fortunate. Let's just say, it's a good thing giving isn't a crime, because when it came philanthropy in 1800s Burlington, Louisa Howard's fingerprints were everywhere.

Born Hannah Louisa Howard in Addison, Vermont on July 2, 1808, she was the fourth child and eldest daughter of John Howard of Providence, Rhode Island and Hannah (Earl) Howard of Bristol, Massachusetts.

Before moving to Vermont, Louisa's father was a sailor, a tavern keeper and had run a mercantile business. In Vermont, he decided to become a farmer and settled his family on land in Addison, near the shores of Lake Champlain. However, city life must have called to him, because, in 1812, he traded in his farm for a Burlington inn and tavern that had been owned by a man named Azra Crane; this was the beginning of his thirty-five-year career as an innkeeper and hotelier. His hotel, which was situated on College Street, between Church and St. Paul Streets, was a busy stagecoach stop. He gained the reputation of being a generous man and landlord who was respectful and fair to his tenants. The newspapers of the day, and at least one chronology of his life, note that he was fondly referred to as "Uncle" John Howard.

The entire Howard family, including "Uncle" John's widowed mother, lived in the hotel. Two of the Howard siblings—Daniel, who was seven years Louisa's senior, and John, who was six years Louisa's junior—ended up pursuing their father's vocation and found their fortunes managing hotels in another state. It seems that the Howard children took to philanthropy naturally. Their father, though not a member of the volunteer fire team called the Boxers, allowed the company, which first met and was organized in his tavern, to house its engine in one of his buildings, and he allowed the company to meet without fee at his hotel for more than a dozen years. John's oldest son, Sion Howard, was a promoter of excellence in the city and a champion of progress, whether it was for railroads or for better schools. He also helped establish Burlington's telegraph company and, like his father, was known for his fairness. It's been written that the former bank teller was the first merchant in town to institute a cash system—previously, merchants had only sold items "on account." He kept prices low and allowed his customers to buy "on time," with only a portion of the money down. He gave liberally to local entities and projects, like the semi-centennial celebration of St. Paul's Episcopal Church; still, his contributions seem slim in the light of those made by his younger siblings.

Louisa and John Purple Howard opened up their wallets to the Queen City over and over again—for both the living and the dead. But for Louisa, giving people handouts and hand-ups became a way of life. She never shirked from a cause that would elevate the health and well-being of the poor and downtrodden, and her close associations with other local do-gooders meant she could multiply her generosity many times over.

Louisa Howard never married and never had children. Some articles claim that she was "an invalid," but that was, perhaps, only in her later years. Her obituary in the *Burlington Free Press*, dated March 26, 1886, indicates that she assisted her father in caring for the sick during the Vermont Erysipelas epidemic between 1842 and 1843, when she would have been in her thirties. Erysipelas is a bacterial skin infection characterized by inflammation and fever; it is also called St. Anthony's fire and can be traced back to the Middle Ages. The disease caused thousands of deaths across the state, but because the name sounded so much like syphilis, many families were hesitant to say much about the cause of a loved one's death.

Louisa has been described as a "friend and benefactor," whose "zealous works on behalf of suffering humanity are worthy of remembrance and emulation." She once sold a prime Church Street property for nearly $9,000 and gave the money to the local mission house on the corner of Pearl and Clark Streets in Burlington—a place that was often the recipient of her good intentions and surplus cash. The organization supplied needy families with food, clothing and medicine, and taught trade classes, like sewing. At Christmastime, the mission would open a "Christmas Center," where mothers of children fifteen years old and younger could, through a system of donations, use "paper money" to shop for gifts that their children would actually prefer as opposed to any item that was offered. Louisa Howard gave additional funds to the project.

Louisa was also on the board of the Home for Destitute Children and was perhaps its staunchest advocate. She donated heavily to the home, which had a goal to give "wretched beggars" an opportunity for "respectability and usefulness in life," and it even made sure that the children who perished while in its care had proper headstones to memorialize them in death. When Louisa's brother John decided to sell his namesake opera house on Church

The Howard family monument. *Photograph courtesy of Thea Lewis.*

Street in Burlington, she talked him into giving it to the home instead. The money was used to fund the purchase and renovation of a Civil War–era hospital in the City's south end, where the home expanded its ability to serve the youth of Burlington. Today, the home is gone; it was morphed long ago into another organization, a non-profit mental health service provider called the Howard Center.

Louisa Howard gave and gave, directing the sum of $500 to St. Paul's Episcopal Church's poor fund, and she endowed the University of Vermont with $5,000 in scholarships for five deserving students—stipulating that they should be "young persons of good morals, good habits and good ability, and obedient to the rules of good order and of the University." After Lakeview Cemetery was opened to the public, it did not escape her notice that there was no chapel for burial services, so she donated $10,000 to rectify the situation. Her giving wasn't all hearts and flowers; while her Christian virtues embraced a "love of humanity," it left no room for layabouts who couldn't or wouldn't pull themselves up by their bootstraps.

Louisa lived to a ripe old age, succumbing to cancer later in life. Struggling physically toward the end, she would often tell people who inquired about her pain, "I am suffering, but happy!" She would also say, "My pain is nothing compared with my Savior's." She was wakeful and talkative the night before her death, and she finally fell asleep at 6:00 a.m. About three hours later, at 9:15 a.m., Louisa breathed her last breath. Her funeral was held at 3:00 p.m. on March 25, 1886, at St Paul's Episcopal Church. She was interred in her family's plot at Lakeview Cemetery.

HOWARD CHAPEL

Architect E.C. Ryer, who designed Lakeview Cemetery, was also chosen to design the cemetery's chapel, which was built by contractor A.B. Fisher. The exact date on which the sanctuary was ready for its first dedication is unknown, but a *Burlington Free Press* article from July 24, 1904, indicates the building was dedicated November 4, 1882.

As the years and decades passed, the little building that was intended, by Louisa Howard, as a refuge for mourners was abandoned by the community. More often, families turned to the comprehensive services that were offered by funeral homes. The chapel fell into disrepair and was

The Louisa Howard Chapel in the fall. *Photograph courtesy of Roger Lewis.*

eventually used for coffin storage during the winters. In 1992, the city even considered using he chapel as an office space. But that all changed when woman named Glenna White, who had driven by the chapel countless times but had never seen it up close, visited Lakeview after the death of her husband. There, she discovered that the distinctive Gothic chapel, with its eight original stained-glass windows, had been closed to the public since 1940. Glenna decided that, instead of flowers for her husband's funeral, she would request mourners to make donations to a chapel fund. In time, Burlington's cemetery commission, and other like-minded volunteers, joined the cause and became the Friends of the Howard Chapel (now Friends of Lakeview Cemetery).

The funds raised by the organization went toward giving the interior a thorough cleaning, replacing the roof, installing radiant-floor heating, restoring the benches and repainting the walls with their original star and flower design. Community activist Jane Ewing, who acted as a liaison between the group and the cemetery commission, and her husband, John Ewing, were energetic advocates for the restoration. In an interview for the Vermont weekly magazine, *Seven Days*, Jane remarked that returning the building and landscaping to its former glory was a "labor of love" for everyone involved.

At the time of this writing, the chapel is available to rent for private services, art displays, meetings, recitals and other public or private events, "as deemed appropriate by the cemetery superintendent." For more information or to reserve the chapel, you can call the office at Lakeview Cemetery at 802-863-2075.

3.

JOHN PURPLE HOWARD

BENEVOLENT PHILANTHROPIST

For unto whomsoever much is given, of him shall be much required: and to whom
men have committed much, of him they will ask the more.
—Luke 28:14

Hotelier John Purple Howard was a Vermont native and a man to whom much was given—in economic advantages, brains, determination and luck. He made a fortune and led a comfortable life, and he used his wealth to improve the lives of others, offering comfort where he could.

John P. Howard was born on June 3, 1814, in Burlington, Vermont, and the hotel business was second nature to him, as his father owned a prosperous hotel and stagecoach stop in Burlington's bustling center. In 1819, John Howard, the elder, gained some notoriety after surviving of the sinking of the steamer *Phoenix*, which caught fire and eventually burned all the way to the water line, near Colchester Shoal, north of Burlington's harbor. After encouraging other passengers to jump and save themselves, John did the same and was found floating on a plank after the steamer sank.

John P. Howard liked to recount how, at the age of fifteen, he left the Queen City, carrying all his worldly possessions in a cardboard bandbox, to join his older brother, Daniel, in the hotel business in New York, near the site of the New York Stock Exchange. He said that, when he entered the hotel, the bottom of the box finally gave out and scattered the embarrassed youth's meager possessions across the lobby floor. The two brothers eventually left the financial district and headed to Broadway and the famous Irving House,

John Purple Howard bust at the Old Mill Building at the University of Vermont. *Photograph courtesy of Thea Lewis.*

a popular performance venue that was once home to the beautiful opera singer Johanna Maria "Jenny" Lind, who was promoted by impresario B.T. Barnum and rose to popularity as the "Swedish Nightingale." In 1840, the brothers took over a six-story hotel, called the Howard Hotel, or "Howard House," on the corner of Broadway and Maiden Lane in Manhattan. With a frontage of 161 feet, and a depth of 130 feet, the hotel boasted a luxurious 130-by-30-foot dining room.

On June 26, 1844, their hotel hosted, in secret, Unites States president John Tyler, who was in town to marry twenty-one-year-old Julia Gardiner, whom the widower had been courting for a while. (History tells us that she hated all of his proposals, including one that he made during a masquerade ball. But she finally agreed to marry him after he kindly supported her at the death of her beloved father.) Word is the brothers had the staff locked up so nobody would spill the beans, and the wedding came as a surprise to the press. The marriage made Julia the youngest first lady in history.

During the final stages of the Civil War—after the hotel had changed hands—a group of eight Southern operatives called the Confederate Army of Manhattan attempted to burn down the Howard, along with eighteen other hotels, a theater and P.T. Barnum's museum. All but one operative escaped prosecution. Robert Cobb Kennedy was arrested the following January while traveling from Canada to Richmond, Virginia. A February 1865 article in the *New York Times* said:

> *Mr. Kennedy is a man of, apparently, thirty years of age, with an exceedingly unprepossessing countenance. His head is well shaped, but his brow is lowering, his eyes deep sunken and his look unsteady. Evidently a keen-witted, desperate man, he combines the cunning and the enthusiasm of a fanatic, with the lack of moral principle characteristic of many Southern Hotspurs, whose former college experiences and most recent hotel-burning plots are somewhat familiar to our readers. Kennedy is well connected at the South, is a relative, a nephew, we believe, of Howell Cobb, and was educated at the expense of the United States, at West Point, where he remained two years, leaving at that partial period of study in consequence of mental or physical inability. While there, he made the acquaintance of Ex. Brig. Gen. E.W. Stoughton, who courteously proffered his services as counsel for his ancient friend in his present needy hour. During Kennedy's confinement here, while awaiting trial, he made sundry foolish admissions, wrote several letters, which have told against him, and, in general, did, either intentionally or indiscreetly, many things, which seem to have rendered his conviction almost a matter of entire certainty.*

John P. Howard retired from the hotel business in 1852 and settled in Long Island, living off his substantial investments and holdings. He traveled extensively but never forgot his hometown. He returned to Burlington often and continued to make his mark on the city in a variety of ways.

The University of Vermont (UVM) had a great champion in Howard. While looking at the campus's buildings, he was bothered that they weren't as prestigious as they ought to be, and he took it upon himself to finance the design and renovation of a handful of structures to enhance their attractiveness and practicality. He funded the construction of a new medical college building and paid for an 1885 facelift of the Old Mill. He also donated the fountain that still sits on the UVM green, and he ponied up the money for the bronze statue of LaFayette that stands nearby. In today's money, Howard paid $25,000 for the statue. Howard also endowed a chair in natural history and zoology department to the

Howard Opera House. *Photograph courtesy of the University of Vermont, Special Collections.*

tune of $50,000. In appreciation of his contributions, the citizens of Burlington gifted a bust of Howard to the university; today, it sits in front of the Old Mill.

In 1878, recognizing that the Queen City lacked opportunities for amusement, Howard financed the construction of the Howard Opera House at the cost of $100,000. The opera house was designed by New York architect Stephen D. Hatch, who conceived many notable structures, including the former New York Life Insurance Company Building at 346 Broadway (also known as the "Clock Tower Building"). Years later, with the building valued at $125,000, Howard's sister, Louisa Howard, talked him into turning over the deed to the manager of the Home for Destitute Children. At the time, it was the largest single gift ever made to a charitable institution in Vermont; in 1881 alone, Howard's charitable gifts totaled $225,000. The Howard Opera House, which was brought to life by local contractor A.B. Fisher, still sits on the corner of Burlington's Church and Bank Streets and is the home of retail and office spaces.

Howard continued to give to the city: a stone chapel for St. Paul's Episcopal Church, fountains to decorate the city's parks and improvements to Lakeview Cemetery. It's estimated that, in all, he donated more than $400,000 to the city of Burlington, and he left an estate of more than $3 million to the city after his death.

By 1885, Howard was living in England in failing health. His friends and relatives in Burlington were shocked, but not surprised, when they received a cable from London, England, saying that he had died suddenly, had already been embalmed and was being transported to Vermont. On October 29, 1885, businesses all over the city closed in respect of the well-known philanthropist. People remarked that the day of his burial was "as quiet as the Sabbath," as windows were draped, and flags were flown at half-mast. In the early hours of the day, friends called at the King Street home of his sister, Louisa, where his body lay, awaiting burial. After a brief, preliminary service that was held at Louisa's home for relatives and close friends, the body was transported to St Paul's Cathedral, where a huge crowd was already assembled. The casket was carried into the cathedral by six members of the Howard Hose Company, one of the city's volunteer fire teams.

Afterward, the youthful residents of the Home for Destitute Children were part of a cortege that followed his remains to Lakeview. The *Burlington Free Press* ventured to say that the procession to the cemetery was possibly the largest in the city's history; it stretched from the cemetery on North Avenue to Battery Park, a mile to the south. The service at the grave was brief and touching. At the very end of the ceremony, students from UVM and children from the Home for Destitute Children filed past the grave to place sprigs of evergreen on the coffin, a last simple and loving tribute to the man who had given them so much. Howard's was the largest private funeral ever witnessed in the city of Burlington.

4

LEANDER AND ISRAEL FREEMAN

BROTHERS OF THE FIFTY-FOURTH

If you've seen *Glory*, the star-studded Hollywood movie that depicts the bloody Second Battle of Fort Wagner that took place in South Carolina in July 1863, then you've seen a depiction of the Civil War soldiers from the Fifty-Fourth Massachusetts Infantry, and you know their story. Two of the soldiers from the Fifty-Fourth are buried in Lakeview Cemetery: Leander W. Freeman, a member of Company F, and his brother Israel. Private Leander Freeman was born in Northfield, Vermont, on August 11, 1841, and Israel was born in Cavendish; their parents were Israel and Clarissa Freeman. They moved to Burlington from Lincoln, Vermont, when Leander was nine years old and Israel was only six. Leander had been working as a laborer in Burlington and enlisted in the Union army on July 13, 1863. Israel, who worked as a butcher, enlisted the following December. (Their brother Coyden Freeman also enlisted that year; he was killed in battle and was buried in Beaufort National Cemetery in Beaufort, South Carolina.)

Governor John A. Andrew of Massachusetts, an abolitionist, issued the Civil War's first call for black soldiers in February 1863. While there weren't many black residents in his state, more than one thousand black men from Vermont, Indiana, New York and Ohio answered his call. (Seventy-one Black Vermonters served in the Fifty-Fourth Massachusetts and another forty-nine served in other units. At this time, Vermont's most recent census put its total African American population at 920 people.) One-quarter of the unit's volunteers came from slave states and the

Caribbean. Some of its most famous soldiers were Charles and Lewis Douglass, sons of abolitionist Frederick Douglass, who played a key role in organizing the Fifty-Fourth Massachusetts.

During the Civil War, every black unit was required to be led by a white officer. While they were fighting side by side with white soldiers to end slavery and injustice, the black soldiers of the Fifty-Fourth Massachusetts were being paid only ten dollars a week, while the white soldiers got thirteen. Ultimately, the entire regiment, including the officers, refused to accept their wages until all enlisted men were paid equally. Congress finally granted equal pay for all soldiers on June 15, 1864.

In the beginning, some were skeptical regarding the assemblage of an all-black regiment, but the regiment's stellar combat record led to an increased recruitment of African American soldiers during the conflict. Their courage through a series of notable battles, especially during the Second Battle of Fort Wagner, finally earned them some of the admiration they deserved. When Confederate general Johnson Hagood buried Union colonel Robert Gould Shaw's body in a common trench alongside his black troops, Shaw's father, abolitionist Francis Shaw, said, "We would not have his body removed from where it lies, surrounded by his brave and devoted soldiers....We can imagine no holier place than that in which he lies, among his brave and devoted followers, nor wish for him better company—what a body-guard he has!"

Israel Freeman seemed like a born leader; he attained the rank of sergeant but was later demoted to private due to his drunkenness. Leander was discharged from the army in 1864, due to the wounds he received in battle, and he returned to Burlington. Israel was present for Lee's surrender at the Battle of Appomattox Courthouse in April 1865, and he returned home to Burlington after the war. An 1868 court report in the *Burlington Free Press* says that he was later cited into court and paid a five-dollar fine for drunkenness.

In 1871, Leander and Israel were living with their mother, Clarissa, at her home, a small two-story house on the eastern corner of Cherry and Battery Streets—Battery was called Water Street in those days. Leander worked as a laborer, and Israel had a butchering business on site that he ran out of the family home. Their mother had also taken in a boarder, a twenty-three-year-old Frenchman named William Carbo, who sometimes helped with Israel's butchering business. Carbo had grown up in the Burlington area. Little is known about him except for court records that indicate several of his younger brothers and sisters were in the care of the Home for Destitute Children.

Leander Freeman's death certificate. *Image courtesy of Ancestry.com.*

On the afternoon of October 26, 1871, Israel saw his friend John Hallahan passing by Clarissa's house and called to him to come and see some new books he'd gotten. Hallahan followed him to the upstairs rooms and found Carbo already there, looking at a box of dime novels. As Israel started to show Hallahan the books, he noticed that one was missing. He had seen Carbo looking at the book and he asked him where it was. Carbo told him he didn't have it. According to Hallahan, Israel Freeman had been drinking and was all at once furious with Carbo, calling him a "son of a bitch" and a liar and telling him he would "fix" him. Freeman lurched toward a basket filled with butcher's knives; he had a reputation of being a mean drunk and had previously, in fits of temper, drawn knives on people. Carbo ran over to stop him, but Israel threw a round-house punch to his head. Carbo punched back, and a scuffle ensued; it ended with Israel Freeman face-down on the floor. Freeman growled at Carbo, "When I get up, I'll murder you!"

Carbo, holding Freeman by the neck, picked up a nearby hatchet and let fly two blows to his skull, literally splitting his head it two. Hallahan, feeling sick, ran for the street and Carbo followed, crying and swearing he would turn himself in, which he did. He went directly to the police office, under the city hall, and told his story to Officer White. Sobbing, he told the man,

"I have killed Freeman. I want you to take me to jail!" Back at the Freeman home, the room filled with curious onlookers. After a few hours, the body was fetched by the superintendent of the poor, who was, at the time, a man named Lowry. Carbo waited a nearly a year for his trial, and he was found not guilty by reason of self-defense. Ten years later, Carbo made the papers again after a long burglary spree. When he was finally captured, he was sentenced to two years in the house of correction.

In May 1892, Leander Freeman married Marion Davis. The couple had one daughter named Hortense. An 1880 census, and Leander's death certificate, list his occupation as "laborer," as he worked in a local lumber yard on Burlington's waterfront. At the time of his mother, Clarissa's, death in August 1893, the *Burlington Free Press* listed Leander's home address as 20 Intervale Avenue, in Burlington's Old North End; he and Marion later moved to 39 Archibald Street. Marion died on April 28, 1913, at the age of fifty-three from Bright's disease, or chronic nephritis, or kidney failure.

Israel Freeman was a member of Standard Post No. 2 of the Grand Army of the Republic, and he was a frequent attendee of services at the local Methodist church. Though, after he died of septicemia on August 20, 1917, his funeral was held at St. Paul's Episcopal Chapel in Burlington. A contingent of the Standard Post No. 2 of the Grand Army of the republic was in attendance, and a quartet sang "Nearer, My God to Thee," "Abide with Me" and "Peace, Perfect Peace," which were his favorite hymns. At his interment at Lakeview, "Taps" was sounded at his grave.

5.

GEORGE JERRISON STANNARD

ALWAYS STEADY

On Memorial Day 1886, while the citizens of Burlington marched and bands played to commemorate the fallen soldiers, Union brevet major general George Jerrison Stannard, the embodiment of the Vermont soldier, lay dying in Washington, D.C. Stannard was born on October 20, 1820, in Georgia, Vermont, about four miles south of the village of St. Albans. He was the sixth son of Samuel and Rebecca (Petty) Stannard and attended public school in nearby St. Albans; his education was later supplemented by secondary instruction at academies in Georgia and Bakersfield, Vermont. His inclination toward a soldierly lifestyle began early; at the age of sixteen, he joined a local militia that responded to frontier disturbances during the Canadian Rebellion. His qualities for leadership and his "cool self-possession," as his obituary in the *Burlington Free Press* put it, served him well for his entire life.

In his late teens and early twenties, like many young Franklin County men of his day, Stannard worked on his family's farm in the warmer months, and in winter, he was a teacher at his district's grammar school. Stannard's parents considered sending him to university, but, while he was described as having "an extraordinarily fine physique," his history of frail health made them overprotective. Instead, Stannard went off to St. Albans, Vermont, just a short distance away, to clerk for the St. Albans Foundry Company. There, he impressed his employers with his efficiency, diligence and ability to problem-solve, as he did on one particular occasion, when he de-escalated a dispute among the company's workers that threatened to turn into an all-out brawl. Within just a few years of his employment at the brick foundry, Stannard was put in charge of operations. In September 1850, he married Emily Clark of St. Albans; they had four children: three daughters and a son. Within ten years, he became a joint partner of the brick foundry.

When the Civil War began, after the confederate attack on Fort Sumter in South Carolina in April 1861, President Abraham Lincoln called for volunteers to join the Union army and George J. Standard was the first Vermonter to answer the call, leaving behind his family and his successful business. When the Second Regiment of Vermont volunteers was organized in May 1861, Stannard was given the rank of colonel but lost the top leadership spot to Captain Henry Whiting, a West Point graduate. Erastus Fairbanks, who was the governor of Vermont at the time, felt that Whiting was better credentialed and had more hands-on military experience. Stannard was later named colonel of the Ninth Vermont Regiment.

Stannard's temperament and reputation for "walking the talk" made him popular with enlisted men. While other officers may have sought creature comforts that were not afforded to their soldiers, Stannard did not. If his regiment was sleeping in a field, he figured his place was with them, not enjoying the benefits of a warm hearth under some nearby roof. It's been written that he was proud of the fact that the promotions he received during his service in the Civil War were due to his behavior, not his political ties. Stannard was described by people who knew him as "frank, blunt, warm-hearted and generous…public spirited and patriotic."

In July 1862, the Ninth Vermont Regiment pressed on to Virginia. On September 15, 1862, during the Maryland Campaign at the battle at Harpers Ferry, Stonewall Jackson's troops captured the Union garrison. The troops were under the command of Colonel Dixon S. Miles, who lacked experience and thought that the situation hopeless. (He was struck by a shell during the battle, which shattered his leg. He later died from complications of this injury.) Stannard urged the colonel to move the garrison to a more defensible position or to attempt a breakout, but his pleas fell on deaf ears. The colonel, against Stannard's vehement protests, saw surrender as their only option. Stannard, unwilling to surrender, attempted a breakout with his regiment but failed. His troops were the last to surrender. Later, when Stannard was asked to sign his men's parole

Harpers Ferry, circa 1861.
*Photograph courtesy of the
Library of Congress.*

papers, he refused, with tears in his eyes; he only acquiesced when the Confederates threatened to imprison him.

More proof of Stannard's leadership abilities followed, and in March 1963, after he managed troops at the Battles of Bull Run and Williamsburg, he was promoted by President Lincoln to the rank of brigadier general. Back in command of Vermont's Second Brigade, Stannard's steadiness and focus on regular and, some said, "relentless" drills, won him the admiration and respect of the five regiments that served under him—as it turns out, the drills weren't just busy work. A previous commander, Brigadier General Edwin H. Stoughton of Rockingham, Vermont, was captured in his bed at his headquarters at Fairfax Courthouse during a raid led by partisan ranger Colonel John S. Mosby; after his capture, Stoughton's appointment, which had not been confirmed, expired. Two months after the infamous incident, Stoughton had still not been reappointed to the position and resigned— Stannard got the post. Life under Stannard's command was a different ballgame. He knew that the men—some still untried—would soon be tested, and he was determined to make them ready. Still, could anyone have really been ready for the Battle at Gettysburg?

Stannard's Brigade left Washington, D.C., on June 25, 1863, intent on joining the Army of the Potomac, which was on the trail of the Confederate forces led by Robert E. Lee. Stannard's troops marched eighteen miles a day for a week to reach their destination: Gettysburg. The battle took place over three days, from July 1 to July. The following is Stannard's official report from the battle.

Report of Brig. Gen. George J. Stannard,
U.S. Army, commanding Third Brigade
O.R.—SERIES I—VOLUME XXVII/1 [S# 43]—Gettysburg
Campaign
HDQRS. THIRD BRIG., THIRD DIV., FIRST ARMY CORPS,
Gettysburg, PA, July 4, 1863
Lieut. Col. C. KINGSBURY, Jr.,
Assistant Adjutant-General

SIR: I have the honor to report that the Second Vermont Brigade, under my command, marched from the line of the defenses of Washington, upon the Occoquan, on the 25th ultimo, under orders to report to Major-General Reynolds, commanding the First Army Corps. The brigade joined that corps at this place on the evening of July 1, after an exhausting march of seven days' duration. The distance marched averaged about eighteen miles per day. The men marched well, with no straggling. Rain fell on every day of the seven, and considering the condition of the roads, the distance traveled (from the mouth of Occoquan to Gettysburg) could not have been accomplished in less time.

We reached the battleground in front of Gettysburg too late in the day to take part in the hard-contested battle of July 1, and my tired troops, upon their arrival, were placed in position, in column by regiments, on the front line, in connection with the Third Army Corps. Before reaching the ground, the Twelfth Regiment, under command of Colonel Blunt, and Fifteenth Regiment, under command of Colonel Proctor, were detailed, by order of General Reynolds, as guard to the wagon train of the corps in the rear. I was detailed, per order of Major-General Slocum, as general field officer, and met Major-General Meade, in company with Major-General Howard, near my command about 3:00 a.m. of the second instant. The Fifteenth Regiment rejoined the brigade in the morning but was again ordered back on the same duty about noon.

On the morning of the second instant, we were allowed to join the First Army Corps and reported to Major-General Doubleday, agreeably to previous orders, and were placed in the rear of the left of Cemetery Hill. After the opening of the battle of July 2, the left wing of the Thirteenth Regiment, under command of Lieutenant-Colonel Munson, was ordered forward as support to a battery, and a company of the Sixteenth Regiment was sent as a support to the skirmishers in our front. While stationing them, Capt. A.G. Foster, assistant inspector-general of my staff, was seriously wounded by a ball through both legs, depriving me of his valuable services for the remainder of the battle.

Just before dark of the same day, the lines of our army on the left center, having become broken under a desperate charge of the enemy, my brigade was ordered up. The right wing of the Thirteenth Regiment, under Colonel Randall, was in the advance, and, upon reaching the break in the line, was granted by Major-General Hancock, commanding upon the spot, the privilege of making the effort to retake the guns of Company C, regular battery, which had just been captured by the enemy. This they performed in a gallant charge, in which Colonel Randall's horse was shot under him. Four guns of the battery were retaken, and two rebel field pieces, with about eighty prisoners, were captured by five companies of the Thirteenth Regiment in this single charge. I placed the Sixteenth, under command of Colonel Veazey, on picket, agreeably to orders, extending to the left of our immediate front. The front, thus established, was held by my brigade for twenty-six hours.

At about 4 o'clock on the morning of the 3d, the enemy commenced a vigorous artillery attack, which continued for a short time upon my position. During its continuance, I moved the Fourteenth, under command of Colonel Nichols, to the front of the main line, about seventy-five yards, which was done at double-quick in good order. I then, with permission from my immediate commander, selected a position to occupy, if attacked with infantry, some distance in front of the main line.

At about 2:00 p.m., the enemy again commenced a vigorous attack upon my position. After subjecting us for one and one-half hours to the severest cannonade of the whole battle, from one hundred guns or more, the enemy charged with a heavy column of infantry, at least one division, in close column by regiments. The charge was aimed directly upon my command, but owing apparently to the firm front shown them, the enemy diverged midway and came upon the line on my right. But they did not thus escape the warm reception prepared for them by the Vermonters. During this charge, the enemy suffered from the fire of the Thirteenth and Fourteenth, the range being short. At the commencement of the attack, I called the Sixteenth from the skirmish line and placed them, in close column by division, in my immediate rear. As soon as the change of the point of attack became evident, I ordered a flank attack upon the enemy's column. Forming in the open meadow in front of our lines, the Thirteenth changed front forward on first company; the Sixteenth, after deploying, performed the same and formed on the left of the Thirteenth, at right angles to the main line of our army, bringing them in line of battle upon the flank of the charging division of the enemy, and opened a destructive fire at short range, which the enemy sustained, but a very few moments before the larger portion of them surrendered and marched in—not as conquerors, but as captives. I then ordered the two regiments into their former position. The order was not filled when I saw another rebel column charging immediately upon our left. Colonel Veazey, of the Sixteenth, was at once ordered to attack it in its turn upon the flank. This was done as successfully as before. The rebel forces, already decimated by the fire of the Fourteenth Regiment, Colonel Nichols, were scooped almost en masse into our lines. The Sixteenth took, in this charge, the regimental colors of the Second Florida and Eighth Virginia Regiments, and the battle flag of another regiment. The Sixteenth was supported in this new and advanced position by four companies of the Fourteenth, under command of Lieutenant-Colonel Rose.

The movements I have briefly described were executed in the open field, under a very heavy fire of shell, grape and musketry, and they were performed with the promptness and precision of battalion drill. They ended the contest in the center and substantially closed the battle. Officers and men behaved like veterans, although it was, for most of them, their first battle, and I am content to leave it to the witnesses of the fight whether or not they have sustained the credit of the service and the honor of our Green Mountain State.

The members of my staff—Capt. William H. Hill, assistant adjutant-general; Lieuts. George W. Hooker and G.G. Benedict, aides-de-camp; Lieutenant [Francis G.] Clark, provost-marshal; and Lieut. S.F. Prentiss, ordnance officer—executed all my orders with the utmost promptness and, by their coolness under fire and good example, contributed essentially to the success of the day.

There were 350 killed, wounded and missing from my three regiments engaged; of the missing, only 1 is known to have been taken prisoner.

I am, with much respect, your obedient servant,
GEO. J. STANNARD,
Brig. Gen.

Stannard was seriously injured during the Battle of Gettysburg when an artillery shell fragment tore open his right thigh, but he stayed on the field until the end of the battle. He was too severely wounded to continue the war effort and returned, temporarily, to Vermont to convalesce. He returned

General George Stannard. *Photograph courtesy of the Library of Congress.*

to duty in 1864, when he joined Major General Benjamin Butler's Army of the James, replacing Brigadier General Charles A. Heckman, who had been captured at Proctor's Creek. As the commander of the First Brigade, Second Division, XVIII Corp, Stannard was wounded again—this time, in the left leg—at the Battle of Cold Harbor, but he continued to lead his troops until Virginia saw the siege of St. Petersburg. At that time, Stannard assumed command of the First Division, XVIII Corps, but at Battle of Chaffin's Farm, while leading the attack on Fort Harrison, he was injured a third time—this time, more critically. His right arm had to be amputated, so he returned to Vermont, where he received a well-deserved hero's welcome. He was assigned light duty for the remainder of the war.

He resigned from the army in June 1866 and worked, for a time, as a customs official in Vermont. In 1881, he began his service as the doorkeeper of the United States House of Representatives. He later wrote from Washington, D.C., to tell his wife that he had not been well, due to a string of "colds." Although he'd seemed an imposing figure during the war, with a strong constitution, his many injuries wreaked havoc on his body. The doctors that attended him near the end of his life recorded that the 5-foot-8-inch-tall general's weight was just 129 pounds. In the end, he contracted pneumonia, which took its toll and killed him in a surprisingly short period of time. Major General George J. Stannard died in Washington, D.C., still in service to his country, on June 1, 1886.

A statue of Stannard can still be seen atop the Vermont memorial at the Gettysburg Battlefield. It was designed by sculptor Karl Gerhardt of Hartford, Connecticut. Mrs. Stannard and her daughters (the couple's son had previously passed away) approved the preliminary portrait of the statue. October 9, 1889, was officially declared as "Vermont Day" in Gettysburg, and Vermonters traveling to Pennsylvania for the event filled thirteen rail cars. Among the citizens who made the trek were then-governor Paul Dillingham, U.S. senator Redfield Proctor and General Edward Ripley, who had been captured with Stannard and the rest of the Ninth Vermont regiment at the Battle of Harpers Ferry.

General Stannard monument. *Photograph courtesy of Roger Lewis.*

General Stannard briefly owned a home in the center of Burlington, at 3 George Street, and it has since developed and remodeled as part of a seven-unit apartment complex. As of this writing, work has begun to restore Stannard's house that was built near Route 7 in Milton, Vermont. The house, which was built around 1840, was added to Vermont's Historic Register in 1980. Even so, the barns, which were built so that a man with only one arm could maintain them, were lost—they were burned as part of a training exercise for the town's fire department in 1989. Preservationists hope to turn the restored landmark into a museum that would honor not only Stannard's life but the lives of the other Vermont figures from the Civil War. The aim is to have the project completed by October 20, 2020, Stannard's two hundredth birthday.

6.

LAWRENCE BARNES

BUILDING BURLINGTON'S LUMBER HISTORY

Lawrence Barnes saved the Queen City—there, it's been said. And, if you don't believe it, you may come away from this story feeling as if he was one of a handful of entrepreneurial visionaries who pointed the city in the right direction.

Born on June 8, 1815, in Hillsboro, New Hampshire, Barnes was from sturdy Pilgrim stock. His ancestor Thomas Barnes had crossed the Atlantic on the historic *Speedwell* that had, in 1656, journeyed with the *Mayflower.* Barnes's parents, Eber and Mary (Adams) Barnes, had seven children; Lawrence was their fifth. Eber was a farmer and a carpenter. His wife, Mary, was a voracious reader, who kept up with politics and current events; this, no doubt, had an effect on the Barnes children—none more so than Lawrence.

Barnes attended local schools. Like most farm children of the day, he contributed to his family's well-being by performing chores around the family homestead. However, at the age of twenty, Barnes was ready for something other than farming. But in those days, children were treated like indentured servants without contracts, and young Barnes owed his father one more year of work. So, Barnes borrowed enough money from a neighbor to pay his father what amounted to a year of time for a hired man, packed a change of clothes and left.

Barnes first went to Nashua, New Hampshire, where he worked for his brother. He labored as a carpenter there for twelve hours a day, and for each day's work, he was paid one dollar. Even though his money was hard to come by, Barnes donated the sum of one hundred dollars, which he paid in installments, toward the building of Nashua's Second Baptist Church. (This was *after* he repaid what he owed his kind neighbor.) He later put carpentry behind him and went to work for J. & E. Baldwin, a company that manufactured spools and bobbins in Nashua. His employers were so impressed by his bright and diplomatic nature that, in a few years' time, they dispatched him to build their new branch in Saco, Maine. On May 20, 1841, Barnes married Lucinda Farmer; together, they had six children. Their family monument in Lakeview Cemetery indicates that three of their offspring died young; their surviving children were named Lawrence K., Georgiana and Ella Frances. By all accounts, the Barnes household was happy and busy one.

Barnes had been employed by the Baldwin brothers for a decade before he decided to go off on his own. With the money he'd saved and a loan of $10,000 from the Saco Bank, Barnes bought ten thousand acres of timberland near the White Mountains, on the Saco River. He later sold half of the property to his former employers for twice as much as he'd paid for it. After that, he was back in business with them, running a lumbering operation. Unfortunately, the business wasn't the success he'd hoped it would be. So, he stayed with the brothers, working in sales for several years, before going off on his own again—this time, buying half of the interest in a lumber business in Island Point, Vermont. However, his partner turned out to be a dud; and in a few months, he was broke and back to square one. But Barnes could not be discouraged; a few weeks later, he purchased, with a promissory note, several million board feet worth of lumber in Three Rivers, Canada. Putting his "carpenter hat" on, Barnes sorted the lumber into lots that were adapted for different building purposes, and he ended up making on the investment three times what he'd originally spent.

Feeling pretty frisky after his success, Barnes contracted with several manufacturing companies in Portland, Maine, to supply them with several shiploads of sugar boxes. The boxes were in great demand when he got the idea, but the demand was suddenly flagged and the lumber and equipment he needed to create the boxes was deemed almost worthless. Barnes was forced into bankruptcy; he sold all of his property for as much as he could, settled up with what creditors he could and promised to make good on the rest. Then, he made another purchase of lumber at Three Rivers and began shipping it, by boat, to Burlington, Vermont, where it was then distributed, by rail, to different points in New England. The year was 1855, and Burlington was a city of about four thousand people—not yet the manufacturing hub it would grow to be. With little business and a railroad industry that was suffering from too many issues and false starts, Barnes was, again, forced to put on his "carpenter hat." He soon figured out a way to dress the lumber before shipping that would save him 12.5 percent in freight expenses—this caused a boom in the local lumber trade. Eventually, Burlington, Vermont, would become the third-busiest port in the nation, due to the volume of lumber that was shipped from its shores. The city was also on a direct route, by water and rail, between the giant forests of Canada and the blossoming cities of the eastern half of the United States. It's been written that in its three most profitable years, Barnes's lumber business made $4 million a year.

But Barnes had other fish to fry; he knew that there were large iron mines in the Champlain Valley, so, with $175,000, he started the Burlington Manufacturing Company, which made nails and other iron products. Based on Barnes's reputation as a successful businessman, others invested in the company, but after two years' time, there were no profits. Operations were suspended, and Barnes, feeling responsible, purchased the other investor's stock, taking the loss. The plant remained empty until, in 1871, Barnes got the idea to turn it into a marble works, which helped the city prosper through the commercial panic of 1873. The marble works became one of the most successful enterprises in northern Vermont.

Then, in 1895, there was a huge bump in Burlington's road to prosperity. The Pioneer Manufacturing Shops on Lake Street, near Burlington's waterfront, were destroyed by fire; the shops had been built on land donated by local businessmen, who intended to rent them out to mechanics and manufacturers to "facilitate and invite the introduction of new branches of mechanical and manufacturing industry" in Burlington. But after the fire, that investment, and a great deal of Burlington's livelihood, was gone. A public meeting was held to figure out how to rectify the situation. Citizens offered a bonus of $8,000 to anyone who would rebuild the shops and equip them for business. Lawrence Barnes not only accepted the challenge (and the bonus), but he finished the project in just ninety days.

Barnes wore many hats once he arrived in the city of Burlington. He was president of the Howard Bank from the time of its organization until his death; he was a stockholder and director of the Burlington Gas Company and the Vermont Life Insurance Company; and he lent his years of knowledge and expertise outside the city's limits, too, to Vergennes's National Horse Nail Company as its president. In 1868, he was elected as one of the directors of the Rutland Railroad Company, and at one point, he was also a trustee of the Vermont Central Railroad. In addition to being a well-regarded businessman, Barnes was a respected politician. He was elected

Pioneer shops in ruins. *Photograph courtesy of the University of Vermont, Special Collections.*

to Burlington's first Board of Aldermen, after the city was incorporated in 1865, and he served in this position for three years. He also represented Burlington in the state legislature in 1864 and 1865, and he was a member of the national Republican convention that nominated President Ulysses S. Grant for a second term. Ever fair, moral and community-minded, Barnes was a long-serving trustee of the University of Vermont and deacon of Burlington's First Baptist Church—he tithed heavily to its coffers.

In April 1866, Barnes purchased the mansion called Grasse Mount— formerly, the Thaddeus Tuttle House—which is situated at the top of Main Street in Burlington. The house was built in 1804, according to plans drawn up by noted architect and surveyor John Johnson. Barnes modified the building by adding a conservatory and a two-story brick ell; he also installed indoor plumbing and coal-burning fireplaces—five on the first floor and four on the second. The previous owners of the home were Captain Charles Marvin and his wife, Ellen Blackman, a Burlington woman. Ellen liked for things to be fancy, and the house was remodeled to her taste; an Italianate belvedere, or cupola, was added to the roof; the windows were replaced to bring in more light; gas lights were installed; wooden fireplace mantels were replaced with Italian marble; and pine woodwork was replaced with black walnut from Spain. Ellen also commissioned multiple, ornate watercolor frescos throughout the mansion's main rooms, stairwell and cupola; they were all hand painted by a professional artist from Italy, who arrived with

Left: Grasse Mount at the University of Vermont. It was the former home of Lawrence Barnes. *Photograph courtesy of the University of Vermont.*

Below: The Lawrence Barnes monument. *Photograph courtesy of Thea Lewis.*

his apprentice and did the work for about $10,000. The paintings included everything, from shoreline scenes, ships and windmills, to palm trees, garlands and cherubs. Lucinda Barnes was none too happy with Ellen's taste, or the painting's "naked images," so she had the artwork covered, except for the ones that had been added to the cupola.

Lawrence Barnes lived at Grasse Mount until his death on June 21, 1886. He had been ill for a long time, and his familiar face had long been absent from the streets of Burlington. During the last few weeks of his life, Lawrence was a different and much less dynamic presence than he had been, and it became apparent that he would never again leave his bed. He died at noon on a Monday.

On the day of his funeral, businesses were closed throughout the city. Stores and mills shut down, and the doorways and interior of the Howard Bank was draped with emblems of mourning. Men wore badges on their right arms to show their respect, and former employees of Lawrence's various enterprises lined up outside of the church, on either side of the street, for several city blocks, in anticipation of his casket's arrival. The interior of the church was draped in black and mourning emblems, and a large, lifelike portrait of Barnes sat in a position of dominance, near the pulpit, surrounded by various floral displays of remembrance. University of Vermont president M.H. Buckham gave a lengthy eulogy, during which he intoned:

> *I said his life was almost the typical life of a self-made man. In one respect, it was not such. The self-made man is almost always self-conscious, self-asserting, of a spirit unlike that of which St. Paul says that it "vaunteth not itself, is not puffed up, doth not behave itself unseemly."*
>
> *There was not, in Mr. Barnes, a particle of this vanity. He was beautifully simple, natural and unconscious of himself. He could not have borne himself more meekly and graciously in the midst of his wealth and his success, if his ancestors for ten generations had had the use and wont of great breeding. He was a native gentleman, one of the truest and best, artless, humble, kindly, incapable of offense, absolutely incapable of malice.*

After her husband's death, Lucinda Barnes remained at Grasse Mount with her sister and a servant. Flowers that had been grown in her conservatory decorated the pulpit of the Baptist church all year long, and she quietly donated money to the church's Sunday school and to the poor. One night, she helped foil a peeping-tom and would-be robber named MacMahon, who was trying to enter her home. She saw him on a ladder, trying to gain access, and gave a perfect description of him to the chief of police. The culprit was found in different clothing, but his quick change was discovered. The habitual offender had already spent time in jail, in Rutland, for breaking into railcars. Lucinda's sharp memory sent him back to familiar lodgings.

Lucinda continued to occupy the home until the fall of 1892, when an illness she'd been fighting turned into pneumonia. A heart condition that she had previously suffered with also played a part in her illness. On

The Lawrence
Barnes monument.
*Photograph courtesy of
Thea Lewis.*

November 4, 1892, with her children gathered around her, she sank into unconsciousness and died just after sunup. Visitors can find Lawrence and Lucinda Barnes, and their children, in the Barnes family plot at Lakeview, marked by a tall monument, which is topped with a striking and inspirational figure of a woman. It has been called one of the most beautiful monuments in Lakeview Cemetery.

7

BRIGADIER GENERAL WILLIAM WELLS

A TALE OF TWO STATUES

When visitors explore the southern side of Battery Park in Burlington, Vermont, they can find a statue on a pedestal, surrounded by a low iron fence. The figure, standing about five foot eight inches tall, is commanding, with eyes that search the distance ahead, as if considering the strategy required for its next move. The figure depicts Brigadier General William Wells, the Medal of Honor recipient who led the troops of the First Vermont Calvary. The statue in Battery Park is a copy of one that was erected in 1913 at the base of the Big Round Top near Plum Creek, in Military Park in Gettysburg, Pennsylvania. The figures were erected to honor Wells, the historic figure who, more than any other this author has encountered, lives up to all of his advance press.

Wells was born in 1837 in Waterbury, Vermont, to William W. Wells and his wife, Elizabeth. His father, a graduate of the University of Vermont, studied law but left the profession to take up a manufacturing position in the town of Waterbury. He married Elizabeth "Eliza" Carpenter, and together, they had ten children, nine of them sons. William Wells was the third child born to the family. He grew up in Waterbury, attended local schools and eventually entered Barre Academy—then, Kimball Union Academy—a private boarding school in Meriden, New Hampshire. While at Barre, at the age of seventeen, Wells showed a talent for surveying and used an odometer to create a map of Caledonia County, an effort that took up two months of his time. By the age of nineteen, he was working in his father's store and showed a keen business sense.

A photograph of the young William Wells. *Photograph courtesy of the Library of Congress.*

But with the beginning of the Civil War, Wells and three of his brothers enlisted in the Union army on September 9, 1861. Wells approached the war in the same way he approached everything else in life, and like most things he did, he aced it, becoming the most-decorated Civil War soldier from Vermont. He attained the rank of first lieutenant in October 1861 and became a captain in November 1861. A year later, he was made colonel, and less than a year after that, on May 16, 1865, thanks to the personal solicitation of Generals George Armstrong Custer and P. Sheridan, he was commissioned as brigadier general.

Through Wells's army career, his quick mind and knack for seeing the big picture made him much admired by peers and commanding officers, and it earned him the reputation of being patient, fair and efficient. He was brave in battle, too; in a moment of quick thinking, after being thrust into a lead role, he led the famous and desperate cavalry charge on Round Top at the Battle of Gettysburg on July 3, 1863.

It is this moment that the statue depicts: The Confederacy had already arrived at the battlefield and had the advantage. The Union army didn't think they had any hope of defeating them, but they decided to do their best to hold the Confederates while the rest of the Union troops made their way to Gettysburg. The intended leader of the charge was General Elon Farnsworth, a twenty-five-year-old who had served with distinction, despite being expelled from the University of Michigan after a drinking party he took part in ended in the death of a classmate (he'd been thrown out a window). Brigadier General Hugh Judson Kilpatrick, who was commanding the Third Division, ordered Farnsworth to make a charge with his brigade against Confederate positions that were south of the battlefield, in an area known as Devil's Den. When Farnsworth disagreed with this tactic, Kilpatrick questioned his bravery, and Farnsworth agreed to make the charge. After being surrounded by the enemy, Farnsworth took multiple gunshots to the chest and was killed. Wells took over, moving his men across the field. They were being attacked by Confederate soldiers from the front and from either side, but, still, they forged ahead, through the Confederate lines, turning them back; then, Wells extracting his troops. It wasn't the complete suicide mission that they had feared. Miraculously, Wells made it through the battle physically unscathed. He later wrote to his parents about the battle:

Dear Parents,

In the afternoon, my battalion B, H, A and G made a charge. Also, the [First West Virginia] *made one on our left.* [General] *Farnsworth led my battalion in the charge. We charged over rocks, over stone walls and fences. Drove in two hundred infantry. Captured thirty or forty prisoners.* [General Farnsworth] *was dismounted. One of* [Company C's] *men gave up his horse to him. The* [general] *was wounded. I have not seen him since. It was reported that he was wounded but in our lines.* [It was not until July 5 that Farnsworth's body was discovered on the battlefield, pierced by five bullets.] *He is a fine officer. We charged about one* [written over with a "2"] *miles until we ran onto a brigade of infantry stationed behind a stone wall in the woods. They opened on us, killed some horses and captured some men. When we fell back, we met Cos L & E & F who were sent to support us....Officers and men behaved themselves gallantly.*

A few days later, in another melee at Boonsboro, Maryland, Wells was cut by an enemy saber, and a few months after that, he was wounded by a shell while charging the enemy's artillery at Culpepper House, Virginia. In all, Wells participated in seventy cavalry engagements, and in eighteen of them, he led a brigade or division. He served in the war continuously from the time he joined the war effort until its conclusion, and he wasn't done serving at the end of the war. Wells was held in "useful service" for eight months after the Civil War was over and was honorably discharged on January 15, 1866. Wells's son-in-law, Horatio Nelson Jackson wrote that he possessed "the highest personal qualities of a cavalry commander, combining coolness, promptness and daring intrepidity with most thoughtful consideration for his men."

Three days after Wells's army career ended, on January 18, 1866, he married his long-time pen pal, Arahanna Richardson, who was called Anna. She was from Fitchburg, Massachusetts, and their correspondence began while she was a student at Kimball Academy, where she was the roommate of Wells's only sister, Sarah. The two had met only briefly before they began to correspond. Wells was twenty-five years old when he sent his first letter to Anna—she was eighteen. In a few months' time, she wrote back, and friendship soon blossomed into romance. The couple had two children: Frank Richardson Wells, born on February 1, 1871, in Burlington, who married Miss Jean Mary Hush of Oakland, California; and Bertha Richardson Wells, born on April 23, 1873, who married Dr. Horatio Nelson Jackson of Burlington, Vermont.

Wells returned to Waterbury after the war, and became a partner in a wholesale drug firm, which moved its business to Burlington and took up residence in the building on College Street that has, for decades, housed a popular gift shop called Bennington Potters North. The drug firm's stained-glass mortar and pestle designs can still be seen above the building's plate glass windows. The company was known for being the manufacturer of the popular Diamond Dyes and an elixir called Paine's Celery Tonic, which it called the "Best Remedy in the World." The tonic's formula was composed of celery seeds, red cinchona, orange peel, coriander seeds, lemon peel, hydrochloric acid, glycerine, simple syrup, water and alcohol. It's rumored that the Wells Richardson Company may have "enhanced" the compound with traces of cocaine. One testimony of the product, written by the wife of a senator, read:

…I was persuaded to try your Paine's celery compound in the early spring, when in a very run-down condition. The duties devolving upon the wife of an official in public life are naturally very exhausting, and I was tired out and nervous when I commenced using the remedy. I take pleasure in testifying to the great benefit I received from its use and can truthfully say that I am in almost perfect health again. If I ever find myself running down again, I shall certainly give it another trial and will, in the meantime, recommend it to everyone needing it.

In Waterbury, Wells served in the Vermont legislature and was a chairman of the military committee. It seemed that whatever post was open in those days, Wells was the right man for the job. He was elected as the adjutant general of Vermont and held the office until 1872. In 1886, he was elected to the Chittenden County seat in the state senate. In addition to the Wells Richardson Company, Wells was a one-term president of the Burlington Trust Company, the Burlington Gas-Light Company and the Burlington Board of Trade. He was also a director of the Burlington Cold Storage Company, the Rutland Railroad Company and Champlain Transportation Company. Wells had the reputation of being one of the

Brigadier General William Wells monument. *Photograph courtesy of Thea Lewis.*

most genial, community-minded men that the citizens of Vermont had ever encountered. He gave what spare time he had to his church, St. Paul's Episcopal Cathedral, as a member and a vestryman, and he was a trustee of the local YMCA.

While it was known that Wells suffered from angina later in his life, his death from heart attack, which occurred during a visit to New York City on April 29, 1892, came as a shock to the Queen City. He was fifty-four years old at the time, and, according to the *Burlington Free Press* article that announced his passing, he had seemed "cheerful and bright" in the time before his death.

His funeral announcement in the *Burlington Free Press* said:

> *…Modest, magnanimous and unselfish, the various public offices he held came to him without his seeking, and others of honor and importance would have been tendered to him, if he had been willing to accept them. He was patriotic and public-spirited. His standard of integrity was a high one. In his private life, he was genuine and estimable; one of the most devoted and affectionate of husbands and fathers; a true friend…*

On the day of his funeral, business was suspended across the city, stores posted photos of the general in their windows and flags flew at half-mast. St. Paul's Cathedral was not large enough to hold the throng that gathered to say goodbye, and the streets outside were crowded with the overflow. The list of government and military dignitaries, businessmen, cadets and factory workers that were in attendance was long. There were so many flowers in the church that the choir and other features of the building were partially obscured—their fragrance permeated air. At the cemetery, the burial mound was completely covered in floral arrangements, evergreen branches, palms and ferns, and at the conclusion of the ceremony,

William Wells statue commemoration, at Battery Park. *Photograph courtesy of the University of Vermont, Special Collections.*

mourners passed to drop even more large clusters of flowers that they had carried to pay their last respects.

In December 1912, governor of Vermont Allen M. Fletcher approved the legislature's proposal to appropriate $6,000 "for the purpose of erecting a monument on the battlefield of Gettysburg." The bronze statue of William Wells was created by J. Otto Schweitzer, who was the artist that created a total of seven statues for the battlefield. Without Wells to model for the portrait, Schweitzer used his actual uniform, boots, belt and revolver as models.

At the commemorative ceremony at Gettysburg, the statue was unveiled by Wells's daughter, Bertha Richardson Wells-Jackson. The statue was so well received that friends of Wells ordered an exact replica to be placed in Battery Park; it is the one that still stands there today.

8

ELIAS LYMAN

THE KING OF COAL

Elias Lyman was born on October 22, 1849, to Elias and Cornelia (Hall) Lyman. He was fifth in a long line of Elias Lymans, and his son was the sixth. He attended local schools, including Burlington High School, before he took up studies at the University of Vermont. Upon his graduation in 1870, Lyman took a job under Senator George F. Edmunds, the husband of his cousin Susan Marsh Lyman and the namesake of what is now Edmunds Middle School in Burlington. As a senator, Edmunds authored a federal statute called the Edmunds Act, which was signed into law on March 23, 1882, by President Chester A. Arthur—it declared that polygamy was a felony. Lyman worked with the senator for a year before taking a teller position at the Merchants Bank, a job he kept until 1874, when he entered into a partnership with Willam H. Wilkins; the two bought half of the interest in a coal company. Later, Lyman went back to banking and became the vice-president of both the Howard Bank and the City Trust Company.

In 1880, Lyman married Harriet E. Phelps of Middlebury, whose father, Samuel E. Phelps, was a United States Senator from Vermont and a supreme court judge; Harriet's mother, Electa (Satterlee), was the senator's second wife. Harriet was described by friends as a warm, intelligent and strong-minded woman. She and Lyman had three children together: Mary, Helen and Elias Jr., who grew up to be a Rhodes Scholar.

When Wilkins retired, Lyman lost no time buying him out and carrying on in the business alone. In May 1893, he formed the Elias Lyman Coal Company on Burlington's College Street. On the streets of Burlington,

Lyman Coal Company office building. *Photograph courtesy of Thea Lewis.*

he became the king of coal. Locals who read the *Burlington Free Press* could not escape his nearly daily print reminders of "COAL! COAL!" An advertisement from September 2, 1891, proclaimed, "Elias Lyman & Co.—Exclusive Agents at Burlington for the Delaware and Hudson Canal Co.'s Celebrated Lackawanna Coal. We also carry in stock the best grades of Lehigh, Cumberland and Clearfield Coals. Car-load lots a specialty." Lyman eventually turned his company into the largest coal firm in the state. As a Republican, Lyman served for four years as the city alderman and for two years as the president of the board.

After the 1910 death of University of Vermont (UVM) president Matthew Buckham, who had served in this role for thirty-nine years, Lyman, a trustee of the university, became the acting president. In this position, Lyman won accolades from the school community and the Burlington community at large for his grasp on the job and his insight into the school's needs during this challenging time. Ever the UVM promoter, Lyman, around 1914, instigated a UVM Founder's Day singing contest, in which the various classes gathered in groups around the statue of Ira Allen and sang college songs, competing for a cup and that year's glory.

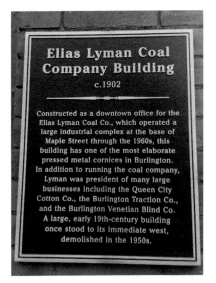

Elias Lyman Coal Company Building

c.1902

Constructed as a downtown office for the Elias Lyman Coal Co., which operated a large industrial complex at the base of Maple Street through the 1960s, this building has one of the most elaborate pressed metal cornices in Burlington. In addition to running the coal company, Lyman was president of many large businesses including the Queen City Cotton Co., the Burlington Traction Co., and the Burlington Venetian Blind Co. A large, early 19th-century building once stood to its immediate west, demolished in the 1950s.

Plaque on the old Elias Lyman Coal Co. building. *Photograph courtesy of Thea Lewis.*

Lyman was a big deal and a part of a group of businessmen who were *all* forces to be reckoned with in the late 1800s and early 1900s. This crowd included Edward Wells, who was a part owner in the Wells, Richardson and Company on College Street and who also served as the president of the Burlington Savings Bank and the vice-president of the Burlington Cotton Mills and the Burlington Safe Deposit Company. Albert E. Richardson, the company's other partner, was described by a *New York Times* reporter as "hav[ing] charge of the proprietary end of his firm's business and draw[ing] checks in the sum of $600,000 worth of advertising." The reporter said Richardson, who was fifty years old, looked more like a forty-year-old man and more like "a prosperous banker or merchant than a 'hustling' adventurer." Lyman's group also included Urban Woodbury, a politician and businessman who owned the popular Van Ness Hotel on Main and St. Paul Streets, and, of course, John J. Flynn of Flynn Theater fame. William James Van Patten, the director of the Queen City Cotton Company, was also a really big deal. He was the president of the Champlain Manufacturing Company, which produced blinds, doors and sashes, and of Burlington's Malted Cereals Company, the creator of the hot breakfast we know as MAYPO. Van Patten, by the way, was the guy who, during his single term as the mayor of Burlington, created the city's first paid fire department and gave the city its first paved streets—pretty impressive. By day, these men ran businesses that were mere city blocks from each other, but when they went home at the end of the day, they were neighbors, living in the South Willard Street "Hill District," in mansions that were all in a row.

Lyman bought a distinctive brick house at 237 South Willard; it's a twin of Hill Hall, the structure at 227 South Willard. The only difference between the two homes was the color of their wood moldings. Both were designed by prominent architect A.B. Fisher, who designed a total of eight homes on South Willard Street. When the Lyman home was put on the market in 1923, it was purchased by Thomas Wright of the Abernethy, Clarkson and Wright department store that existed for decades on Burlington's Church Street. The building is now named Lyman Hall and is part of the Champlain College campus. Like many of Burlington's businessman, Lyman was a member of local social organizations, including the Algonquins, and the Ethan Allen Club. When he died, he was one of the four oldest living members of the Washington Lodge of Masons.

On May 19, 1915, after thirty-five years of marriage, Lyman's wife, Harriet, suffered a heart attack at midnight at the Hotel Del Prado in Chicago—she did not survive. The Lymans were visiting the Windy City with their daughter Mary, to attend the wedding of their son, Elias Jr., and his fiancé, Miss Dorothy Dewhurst. At some point after the nuptials, the newly married pair left for their honeymoon and headed in the direction of the Green Mountain State. Upon their arrival in Vermont they learned of Harriet's untimely death and cancelled the plans for their trip. Elias Lyman died on Saturday, March 31, 1923, at the age of seventy-three. At the time, he was the president of the Burlington Traction Company and the Military Post Street Railway company; J.J. Flynn was elected to fill those roles. As for the Elias Lyman Coal Company, it lived on and became the Elias Lyman Coal and Oil Company in 1951. In the 1980s, when it was known simply as Elias Lyman Oil, the company was sold to Ultramar, an eastern Canadian gas and home fuel retailer with head offices in Montreal, Quebec.

9.

CHARLES HEYDE

A MOST TEMPERAMENTAL ARTIST

Renowned landscape artist Charles Heyde is not buried with his wife, Hannah, which is just as well; the two had a fraught relationship when they were alive, and there's probably no good to be found in extending it into the afterlife. Heyde was a complicated man, as many artists are; he was troubled, drunken, jealous and abusive.

It is presumed, though no one knows for sure, that Charles Louis Heyde was born in 1822, in France, as the son of a sailor, a captain who died at sea. He was raised in Philadelphia, and when he was a young man, he moved to Hoboken, New Jersey, and, later, to Brooklyn, New York.

In the early 1850s, he was a successful artist and exhibited works at the Pennsylvania Academy of Fine Arts and the National Academy of Design in New York. At that time, through social circles, he met poet Walt Whitman, and in 1851, he began boarding with the Whitman family, where he spent time in close proximity to Hannah Louisa Whitman, the poet's pretty, gray-eyed younger sister. Hannah was, by all accounts, Walt Whitman's favorite sibling. They had both been teachers, and it's been written that she was the only member of the family who really understood and appreciated his writing. Whitman encouraged the relationship between his sister and his friend—something he would come to regret. The pair was married in 1852 and traveled north, to the Green Mountain State, settling for a time in Rutland. Heyde was looking for fresh material, and as a painter of the Hudson River School, he took much of his inspiration from nature. He ended up falling in love with Vermont. Hannah, however, was homesick

Heyde landscape of Mount Mansfield. *Photograph courtesy of the University of Vermont, Special Collections.*

and miserable over their impoverished lifestyle. It couldn't have helped that Heyde was constantly traipsing off in search of artistic inspiration, leaving Hannah with little or no resources and to fend for herself in, what felt to her, a strange place.

In 1854, after moving to a series of small, isolated towns in pursuit of Heyde's inspiration, the couple landed in Burlington. There, he set up a studio at the corner of Maple and Battery Streets, in the Rutland and Burlington Railroad Company depot, where he offered renderings of the Adirondacks, Shelburne Bay and other familiar local scenes. He developed a wealthy clientele and moved to Church Street, which was becoming the city's new commercial district. Throughout his career, there were three Vermont subjects that Heyde painted over and over again: Mt. Mansfield, the High Bridge over the Winooski River and Lake Champlain. These scenes, whether they were depicted in spring, summer, fall or winter, were favorites among his customers and always delivered a lucrative outcome.

Heyde liked to surround himself with the colors of nature, even while indoors. James P. Hickok, a Burlington city clerk of the time, wrote an account of his visit to the artist's studio.

Enter the fine building on Church Street called Allen's Block, ascend the stairway and pass to the extremity of the long, narrow passage, where a sign points to a door on the left labeled "Studio"....The ceiling, or sky, as the artist himself designates it, is painted a certain shade of blue; a green paper tones the wall; the floor is of the hue of near seas.

In 1862, Hannah wrote her mother during one of Charles's nature-seeking absences.

Sunday Evening Sept [21, 1862]
Dear Mother,

I rec'd [sic] *your kind letter. I was anxiously expecting it, I am more than ever anxious now to hear from home. Soon as you hear, dear Mother, that George is safe, you must write or telegraph immediately to me, perhaps you have heard, and I shall get a letter tomorrow. You are kind to write to me so quickly, I appreciate it; I cannot write about or tell you anything untill* [sic] *I hear from George, don't fail to let me know. I feel anxious. I have been very ill but feel well today. I have not been out since I went to mail the last letter I wrote to you. I have not been downstairs for some time. I have boarded with, or the people living downstairs have brought up my meals for a week and more, now I shall do for myself, again. I would board with them untill* [sic] *I got strong if they were willing, but they do not seem so disposed. They have been kind since I have been sick. I did not want much, however, they have plenty of help. I have now a very skilful* [sic] *doctor. I should not have been so ill, if the* [doctor] *I had previous had not neglected me. Dr. Thayer is just as kind as possible for anyone to be. I have been acquainted with him a long time; almost the only thing of much benifit* [sic] *is for me to be quiet, not take any exercise at all, Dr. Thayer says*
I can be helped much, but it will be years before I get well. I don't think so at all. I have enlargement of the womb (and falling). I know I shall get well soon, dear Mother. I have said many times, if George was only safe, I would not complain. Let me know, dear Mother, just as soon as you hear—I get along nicely here alone, do not feel the least anxious about me—I cannot think of anything now but about George.
I will write again just as soon as you write and let me know.
Charlie will be home soon. He sent me some beautiful presents from Canada. I did not wish him to know I was so ill. He is engaged on a picture that he is much pleased with the subject. I wished him to be successful and not to be annoyed with any care. I have often wondered why Walt did not write to me. Give my love to all, dear Mother. I have often

wished Jeffy would send me his wife and child's pictures. Tell Matty I hope to see her someday and that I have thought many times this summer, if I was only well, how I would like to have her and little [sister] come and stay some weeks with me. I could have made it pleasant. Give Andrew and his wife my love. I am anxious to have his baby named George. I intended in my last letter to ask permission [sic] to name it. I have written, dear Mother, as I always [do to you] in a hurry. I shall have to depend on someone to carry this to the office. Write, dear Mother, and tell me George is safe. Much love.

Good night,
Han

I shall come home some time, dear mother? I could not now, but I am permanently better shall soon be strong.

In 1862, Heyde had reached what was likely the pinnacle of his career. He won a design competition that was sponsored by the Vermont Historical Society, which was searching for an artist to reimagine the Vermont coat of arms. The prize money for the competition was fifty dollars, a decent sum in those days. Unfortunately, the work disappeared at some point and was replaced in 1898 with a work from another painter, W.C. Stacy.

While in public, Heyde played the part of an accomplished and successful artist, but his domestic life was in turmoil. His wife missed her home and family in New York, and she was treated terribly by Heyde, who denied her creature comforts and even medical care in favor of his desire for a strong drink. At one point, she needed dental care, but he resisted giving her money for an appointment. Eventually, he offered the dentist a small portrait as payment but resenting having to do so. Many of the letters Hannah wrote to her brother and mother told of Heyde's shoddy treatment of her. Some were written in pencil, because Heyde wouldn't even allow her the puny sum she needed to buy ink—some were smudged with teardrops.

Hannah had gone from being the prized and doted-on youngest sister in the Whitman family, to being the physically assaulted and berated wife of Heyde. Whitman wrote to a friend about the situation: "That whelp, Charlie Heyde, always keeps me worried about my sister Hannah: he is a skunk—a bug....He has led my sister hell's own life: he has done nothing for her—never: has not only not supported her but is the main cause of her nervous breakdowns."

In 1865, the Heydes bought a home on Pearl Street in Burlington, and Charles set up his studio there. Living and working in the same place, day in and day out, did not improve the couple's relationship. Heyde had his complaints about Hannah, which he shared in letters to her brother.

Burlington
April 1866

Walter Whitman,
Your letter to Han was recd [sic] *and duly deliverd* [sic]. *She is, I think, better than for a long time past. Only one new vargary* [sic] *has originated with her, and that is that I shall go away; rent the house to her, and she will take boarders; there is but one step from this to insanity—*

Han has an idea that she could accomplish that for three or four persons, easily, which she has, under no circumstances, done for me, not ten times in as many years. I have just taken up a note against the property, and I think that, with reasonable success, I may clear it all by next spring. But the idea that Han runs the house and I am but the secondary drudge must be dismissd [sic].

I see but one way to bring this matter into a realizistic [sic] *shape or condition, and that is to take her at her word; "to go away" and put the place and herself under the guardianship of an attorney.*

Much of this difficulty has arisen from the miserable teachings of her mother, who enjoined upon her when we were first married, not to perform these little services for me, which naturaly [sic] *would suggest themselves to a kind and considerate wife and endear her to her husband: Because I might be spoild* [sic] *by it.*

Mrs. Whitman has been, toward me, a silly old woman—for why, I do not know—I never was under obligations to her for anything. If she brought a half loaf of bread to my house, she took butter or tea away in return for it, and I never had a meal at her table that I did not pay for. But Mrs. Whitman never did possess a particle of honest frankness—on the contrary, in one instance, I will not her[e] mention, a more than mean, a wicked duplicity toward myself.

Perhaps I would not look upon Leaves of Grass with so much melancholy regard if I was not experiencing a practical version of it: Irregular—disorderly: indifferent or defiant—the lower animal instincts—no accountability, no moral sense or principle—no true, inherent, practical sympathy for anything; myself; disappointments, or endeavours [sic]. *Nothing of me, or of the future to arise for me, out of my labour and progressions.*

Han has no more moral sense of marriage than an Ethiopian, of the field—gives herself to a man and nothing more—Your letters and those of her friends shall be allways [sic] *forwarded to her. I am simply disgusted with so much selfishness.*

C.L. Heyde

There is one more change, to the last notion of Han's, and that is "She" can go "home," and cook for her mother: "her mother said so." She sometimes says that she has no friends. I believe it, since this "home" is offrd [sic], *in a menial capacity, and the service that is imagined can be extracted from her. My idea was that, if I did go to Europe, "to let her board, in the most comfortable manner, and raise herself from ill health and drudgery—*

To supplement his income, Heyde began teaching drawing at the Burlington Female Seminary. He also offered painting classes in watercolor and oil for an additional ten dollars per pupil. Ultimately, he found work with local photographers A.G. Styles and L.G. Burnham, colorizing their photos. His landscape paintings began to take on a slapdash look; they were created over a few days' time, instead of over a week. They weren't bringing in the money they did before. Hannah wrote to her brother, trying to cast a cheery light on the situation.

Sunday Evening, November
Dearest Brother,

Your book came last night. I was just delighted. I prize it greatly. I shall always keep this one—every single one of the others are gone, the last one you sent Charlie also, and he lent them to his friends, and that's the last of them. I said last night that this one does not go out of this house under any consideration as long as I live.

Don't you think it's got up finely—I do.

It will be sucessful [sic], *many speak of it here. We looked it over all the evening, Charlie taking it, then I. He read aloud (appreciatively) the "Song of Myself." I wanted to read the "Ox Tamer" and others I liked. There is something so touching or affecting in the words, or title, "Sobbing of the Bells," (you know you sent to Boston Globe), we were so taken with and*

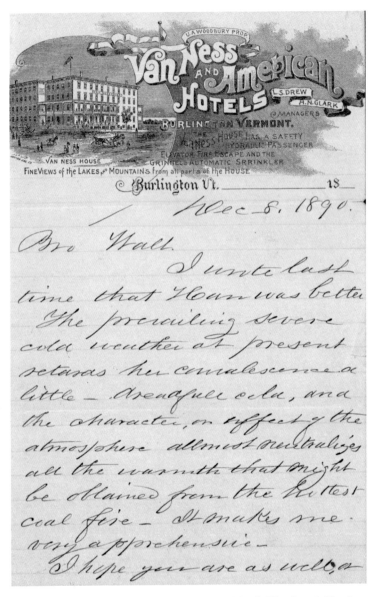

Heyde's letter to Whitman on stationery from Urban's Woodbury's Hotel.
Photograph courtesy of the Whitman Archives.

glad to get read the rest of the poem. Charlie sits here, reading your book, he says this book is electrick [sic]. You can't immagine [sic], Walt, how many speak of you to me. I believe everybody under the sun knows of you, even persons that live far back in the country. The other day, a lady friend Mrs. Barney called that lives back among the Richmond Hills, away from any village, among other things, she spoke of a full-length picture of you having been painted for a German Club out West, all have something to say of you that is pleasant for me to hear.

Some want to see me, Walt Whitman's sister. I have not begun to put on airs yet, but I don't know but I shall soon.

I was pleased with Mr. Luce, a Wisconsin editor that called some months since. He has sent us several of his papers, most all speak of you. I don't know that you would care for it, but I will send you the first one.

Mrs. Abbott (an old, very intelligent friend that we had not seen for twelve years, used to live here) called yesterday. She wanted your new book, should purchase it here if she could, or wait till she arrived in Boston—I said I would tell you that she wanted you very much to visit her at their farm among the mountains, spoke of many things she would do for you if you would come. I told her you had promised to come here some time.

Walt, I am ashamed I did not write last spring when you sent me that money. You understand how much I do appreciate it. For a day or two, I could only think how good you was. And then, I never in all my life had money that done me so much good. I have some of it yet. I saved to finish out a dress I wanted for this winter. This dress will be all that I shall need. I don't know whatever I should do without you, Walt. In many ways, always some pleasant surprise [sic], a paper or magazine letter something or other, all so pleasant to get. Life would be dull without you.

That West Hill letter. I think perhaps I know more of those places you describe than the rest of the family, so to me, it was more than interresting [sic] something to keep. Charlie wrote a pleasant letter to Dr. Bucke Canada. Got a kind letter in reply, spoke of you and he taking dinner together in New York, but the best was that you was pretty well. Your [November 1] letter, too, said you was well as usual. I am so glad, after all the work, and worry you must have had. But, sometimes, we take long walks in the country, we went today, a mile or so.

Charlie has been sketching some this summer out Williston, eighteen or twenty miles from here. We drove out there two weeks ago, the country was beautiful. I liked the ride ever so much.

He has sent his Williston picture West, he thinks it sold, he will know soon. He sold one there previous for $75, has just now sold a small one $16. He has some prospects. We have ups and downs, like everybody. He sold more years ago than late years. I think his pictures much better now, people here follow the fashion, buy foreign pictures

I am well. I feel better than I did last summer. I worry less if things go crossways. Dear, dear brother, I hope to live long enough to see you again. I want you to come here more than I can say.

What a lovely time you must have had in Boston, Walt, socially, I mean. Your long letter was delightful to get, told me so much your dinner at Emerson's and all the rest. I remember I thought you was good to think of me. How many good friends you have, it was all just splended [sic].

I like Dr. Bucke. I feel flattered to be ever so little like Mrs. Bucke.

The Burlington Free Press says you are going to Europe this fall. There is no truth in it, is there? I noticed your [long] poem, "Song of the Banner at Daybreak," in Free Press a while ago.

With me, dear Bother, everything goes much the same. New neighbors about us, with one exception, [General] Henry, I liked the old ones best.

I run in Mrs. Griswold's, one of our neighbor's, a good dead, she very often speaks of you.

If you should build that little house, Walt, you used to speak of, I shant forget that old invitation. I am sorry it's so late. I can't write to Lou. I wanted to, so she would write to me. Ever so much love to you, dear Walt and George and Lou and Eddy. I very, very often think of him.

Good night,
Han

In 1872, there was an interesting marketing ploy at the American Hotel on Burlington's Main Street; it included a raffle of Heyde's painting "Devil's Chute." The painting had been in an exhibit for several weeks, and at the time of the draw, tickets were still available.

Whitman sent books and money, five and ten dollars at a time, to Hannah, even though he was often struggling financially. Neighbors even took pity on the pair, offering money and food. Turning more and more to drink, Heyde fell apart. He'd often set off from home toward the city center, carrying his slipshod work and hoping to trade with a local grocer or coal merchant. Hannah's brothers sent more money, trying to help keep the household going; all the while, her husband's tirades grew louder and more frequent.

In the end, Heyde, who was already suffering from alcoholism, developed dementia. He was committed to the Vermont State Asylum in Waterbury, where he died in 1892. He and Hannah were childless, and Hannah either didn't have the cash to buy a stone or didn't care. Heyde was buried in an unmarked plot in Lakeview Cemetery. Modern visitors to Lakeview Cemetery may never expect that such a talented artist lay in Heyde's unadorned grave. Luckily, the Chittenden County Historical Society placed a stone there to honor him in 1987.

Hannah died in 1908, sixteen years after Heyde's death. She was not buried beside her husband but in her family's plot in Harleigh Cemetery in Camden, New Jersey. While thousands had gathered for the interment of her brother, Walt Whitman, the only people in attendance of Hannah's entombment were her niece, Jesse Whitman; Colonel Porter H. Dale, who conducted the service; and the undertaker's assistants, who acted as pallbearers.

10.

SOCRATES BEACH

A FORTUNE IN COOKIES

S ocrates Beach was born in Westford, Vermont, on July 10, 1823. He took advantage of what local educational opportunities were available to him in those days, and at the age of eighteen, he parted ways with his hometown, intent on a different life in the city of Burlington. A few years after his arrival in Burlington, he began working in a bakery at the corner of Main and South Water Streets (what we call Battery Street today). The bakery was owned by General Joseph Hatch of New Hampshire. Beach later met the general's oldest daughter, Abigail, and married her.

In 1862, at a time when all of Burlington's firefighting teams were made up of volunteers, Beach became a fire assistant for Burlington's District 1. They were a brave and competitive bunch, battling dangerous and fast-breaking fires without the technology that fire crews have today. Beach's family grew; he and Abigail had two sons, Joseph and Charlie, and a daughter, Harriet. Beach, a relatively private person, led a family-oriented life. He never sought public office but did serve the local Methodist church for more than twenty years as its treasurer. When it came time for Abigail's father to retire, Beach bought his bakery.

In 1861, the Confederates bombarded Union soldiers at Fort Sumter in South Carolina—Beach did not rush to enlist. And while he didn't serve in the war, he was still a part of the war effort; he regularly raised the spirits of the enlisted men with large donations of baked goods. An October 17, 1862 *Burlington Free Press* article reported:

Three Cheers for Beach!
Just as the Twelfth Regiment were about to take cars for New haven, a barrel of cookies and other nice articles in the bakery line came to hand; a present to the Howard Guard by our townsman, Socrates Beach, Esq. The sight and distribution of the contents of the barrel produced lively pleasure among the soldiers, and three cheers for the generous donor were given with a will.

In 1867, disaster struck. The wing of the S. Beach Bakery building on Main and Water Streets, the area of the bakery that housed the ovens and other machinery, caught fire. The building could not be saved, but Beach's storehouses survived, and his loss was covered by insurance. He later moved his business to 198–202 College Street and expanded. His three-story bakery in the "Brick Block" was the first wholesale baking company in the city. Beach further distinguished himself and his product when he chose to make his own yeast from potatoes, instead of buying it. The women in the Burlington community took advantage of this resource and sent their children, small buckets in hand, to buy Beach yeast.

The expanded S. Beach Company produced cookies, breads and other treats. The factory's menu items that were featured in an 1868 issue of the *Burlington Free Press* (on the same page as an advertisement for dentistry) included, but were not limited to, graham crackers, wine crackers, seed cakes, African jumbles, Naples biscuits, lady fingers and a frosted Washington loaf cake. The company was one of the first cracker manufacturers in Vermont. People loved the distinctive, savory-sweet flavor of his Burlington crackers, and the company soon began shipping them all over the world—even as far away as India. As his business grew, Beach made smart investments; his holdings included some of the most valuable real estate in the city—much of it on Church Street, the city's blossoming central business district.

In his later years, Beach delighted in taking part in the Christmas Eve entertainment for the charges from the local Home for Destitute Children. The waifs were bundled into huge, four-horse sleighs, given a tour of the city and brought to a stop at Beach's College Street business to load up with cakes and cookies for the ride home.

Before Beach died of a heart ailment in 1904, at his home on Maple Street, he had drawn up a will and chosen an executor, but he hadn't anticipated the early deaths of some of his heirs. This created a swirl of confusion over the dispersal of his wealth. There was even a situation in which Beach's daughter-in-law (the second wife of his widowed son, who he married after

The Socrates Beach monument. *Photograph courtesy of Thea Lewis.*

Beach's death) claimed she was owed her predecessor's place in the will. An early glimpse into the kerfuffle was captured in the *Burlington Free Press* on February 18, 1926.

Heirs Claim that Trustee of Socrates Beach Estate is too Parsimonious

Another case of appeal from the probate court in the trust estate of Socrates Beach, late of Burlington, was filed in county court yesterday. An appeal taken to the chancery court and heard by Judge Julius A. Wilcox at the September term, 1925, was dismissed. In the present case, Joseph T. Beach and his wife, Mary L. Beach, are the appellants, while Elihu B. Taft of this city, trustee of the Beach estate, is named as the appellee.

It is alleged that Mr. Taft failed to allow the claims for medical care for Mary L. Beach, who is said to be in poor health and is in a sanitarium in this city. The appellants say that the will of Socrates Beach provided that the wife of Joseph T. Beach should receive funds for such medical and other care. The wife mentioned in the will was Cora E. Beach, but the appellants state that the provision was made that, in case of her death and the remarriage of Joseph T. Beach, the second wife should receive the benefits of the provision. Mary L. Beach is the second wife.

The case was dismissed in probate court, January 11, 1926. Mr. Taft, the trustee, has filed with the probate court his statement of the case. He says that he declined to provide medical attendance because he believed that Mrs. Beach has large sums of money saved from the funds which he had already previously paid to her.

Mr. Taft also states he is now paying Emma Beach Hazelton, one of the beneficiaries under the will of Socrates Beach, $75 per month, paying Joseph T. Beach $75 per month, and paying Mary Beach $25 per month. He says that the net income of the estate does not suffice to pay more than these amounts.

The appellants claim that, had the estate been properly handled, there would be funds sufficient to do what they are asking.

They ask in their petition that the probate court require Mr. Taft to render a detailed account more adequate than that already rendered of the funds received and expended in connection with the estate…

What followed was decades of suspicion, drama and a string of litigation that wasn't fully resolved until the spring of 1970, when the remainder of the Beach estate was finally distributed to Beach's three surviving great-grandchildren. Sixty-six years, four executors and a handful of court rulings and reversals later, S. Beach's accounts were finally settled.

11.

MAJOR GENERAL
OLIVER OTIS HOWARD

CHRISTIAN SOLDIER

Oliver Otis Howard was born in Leeds, Maine, the son of Roland Bailey Howard, a farmer, and his wife, Eliza (Otis). As the oldest of five children, Howard lived with his family in a large, two-story frame house that owned by his grandparents, Captain Seth Howard and Elizabeth (Stanchfield). The home sat on roughly eighty acres that boasted cows and oxen, sheep, turkeys, hens, gardens and an apple orchard. The homestead had gotten to be too much for the elder Otises to handle, so the younger couple moved to Leeds to lend them a hand. While Howard's grandfather couldn't do the heavier work, he did pitch in, giving Roland time to make extra money in raising, training and selling horses—it was something he was good at. He was so good, in fact, that he was able to clear the farm of its financial obligations much sooner than he had anticipated.

For a while, Oliver Otis Howard had an idyllic life, playing on the farm and listening to his adored grandfather's stories about the Revolutionary War. His grandmother, a devout Christian, no doubt had a huge influence on the moral compass that would serve Howard throughout his life.

At the age of four, Howard began attending the district school, and when he turned six, his father visited family in Troy, New York, and returned with Edward Johnson, a young black boy who was about Howard's age. Edward lived with the Howard family for four years, and the two became friends. According to Howard, they toiled on the farm together, but they also played marbles, flew kites, skated and played ball, like other boys would. Howard later wrote that he believed this early experience relieved him "from that feeling of prejudice which would have hindered [him] from doing the work for the freed-men, which years afterward was committed to [his] charge."

On April 30,1840, when Howard was just nine years old, his father hemorrhaged and died while sitting in church. Two years later, his mother married a prosperous farmer named Colonel John Gilmore, who had children of his own, and the family moved six miles away from the only home that Howard had ever known. On top of this, despite the help of a hired hand who had worked under his mother's supervision, Oliver had considered himself something of the "man" in the family, and he was none too happy to be taken down a peg or two by his stepfather's youngest boy, who was a few years his senior. That fall, before Howard's eleventh birthday, he was sent away to go high school. There, he lived with the family of his mother's brother.

Oliver attended three schools, all named after the towns in which they were located: Monmouth Academy, North Yarmouth Academy and Kents Hill School. He studied doggedly, and at the age of sixteen, he entered Bowdoin College. That same year, he met the girl who would become the love of his life: Elizabeth Ann Waite of Portland, Maine. She was just fifteen years old. Howard graduated in 1850, at the age of nineteen, and turned his attention to the United States Military Academy at West Point, an opportunity that was available to him because his uncle John Otis was serving as a congressman for the state of Maine at the time. Howard claimed that his "favorite companion" while he was a cadet at West Point was Henry W. Closson from Whitingham, Vermont, who was a poet and "very quick-witted."

Howard graduated from West Point in 1854; he was the fourth in his class of forty-six cadets. He later became a mathematics professor at the academy. The year after his graduation, Howard applied for a twenty day leave of absence to marry Elizabeth, which he did on Valentine's Day. The wedding was held at the home of his bride and her mother, Mrs. E.B. Waite. His autobiography recalls, "Every necessary arrangement was made for a private wedding, but as the relatives on both sides were numerous and intimate friends were not wanting, Mrs. Waite's apartments were soon filled with a happy company." The only bit of friction during the wedding came from Mrs. Waite, who said her son-in-law's full-dress West Point uniform, with sash and belt, made the occasion seem "too much like war."

As a newlywed, Howard moved between posts in Troy, New York, and Augusta, Maine, and he was later assigned to Fort Brooke, near Tampa, Florida. Howard, a born family man, missed Elizabeth and his infant son, Guy. In late August 1857, Howard received orders to return to West Point, where he began his career as a math professor. He also acted as superintendent of the West Point Sunday school for the children of the enlisted men. He was considering a career change—mulling over becoming a minister—but his wife disapproved. Then, in 1861, the Civil War came calling. Howard answered, telegraphing Governor Israel Washburn Jr. and offering his services after he heard President Lincoln's call for seventy-five thousand Northern soldiers to put down the "Southern Insurrection." Upon hearing this, James Gillespie Blaine, the speaker of the Maine House of Representatives, asked if Howard would

General Oliver Otis Howard.
Photograph courtesy of Bowdoin College.

have any interest in leading a regiment that was forming in the Kennebec region—he said he would.

But Howard made a terrible first impression. The men felt that Howard talked down to them, and they hated his sermonizing. They voted him in as colonel, despite the tone of his addresses, like this one: "There are two things that I hate. The one is drunkenness and the other is profanity. I set my face against them and shall do it. I loathe these two things. They are the worst enemies we have to encounter; for profanity sets us as rebels against God, and drunkenness makes us worse than rebels at home." (He was from Maine, after all, the first state to try Prohibition, thanks to Portland mayor and Quaker Neal Dow. Dow famously passed, in 1846, the "Twenty-Eight Gallon Law," which prohibited the sale of alcohol in less than twenty-eight-gallon quantities to all but doctors.)

Despite the initial negative impression of Howard, he was a decent commander, if not a great one. He served at the First Battle of Bull Run, the Battle of Seven Pines, Sherman's March to the Sea, the Carolinas Campaign and the Battles of Chancellorsville, Gettysburg, Chattanooga and Atlanta. At Chancellorsville, Howard's corps was almost wiped out when he didn't pay attention to a warning that he'd gotten beforehand. At the First Battle of Bull Run and the Battle of Fair Oaks, he was shot twice in his right arm, and it had to be amputated. Otis was right-handed, but he wrote to Elizabeth with his left hand to let her know that, despite his injury, he and his brother, Charles, who had been grazed in the thigh, were doing all right.

[June 3, 1862]
Head Qrs. Str.
Nellie Baker
"White House Landing"

Dearest,

I am on my way with only my left arm. Shall go to Fort Monroe today and probably to Baltimore
tonight, but maybe I shall wait for a [streetcar] *going directly to* [New York] *from Ft. Munroe, to avoid changes. Charlie is very comfortable and so am I. God bless you and the children. Shall see you soon.*

Affectionately,
Yr [sic] *husband*

Howard wrote to his wife and children as often as he could. Their responses, like this one from his eldest son, Guy, who was just nine years old at the time, must have been a welcome diversion from the war. The letter below mentions a pony that was delivered by Guy's uncle, Charles H. Howard, and George Washington Kemp, a former slave who was helping Howard's widowed mother, Eliza Gilmore, on her farm.

Dear Papa,

I began a letter to you last Sunday and did not finish it, now will copy that first then write more. I thank the officers very much indeed for my pony. I could not have received a better or a nicer present. It is just what I have been wanting so long.

Wash is a very nice man and takes good care of my pony. I donot [sic] *know what to name the pony. I have been on him three times; once, I went as far as Capt. Tuners. I don't go alone; Wash leads him. The pony likes to play and stand up on her hind feet and put out her fore feet towards Wash. Grace and I are teaching Wash to read. I hope he will stay with us a long time. I am glad you got all my letters before you left Savannah.*

Mother thinks you may not get these letters for some time. Jammie says he must have a letter from Papa soon.

No one went to church last Sunday; the roads were not broken out; we had a very plesent [sic] time at home. Uncle Charly was here; he is coming home from Farmington to-morrow [sic] in the train.

Today is very plesent [sic]. Grand-mother [sic] and the girl and the hired man went to church. It is now half past four. Capt. Tuner has just come in. Chancy and Jammie are sitting in his lap. Wash would like you to give his respects to Sam and tell him that he is well.

Please give my love to Dr. Duncan. I just read your letter aloud to Mother. Are you going to bring that nice horse home that was given you on the march? This letter will go tomorrow with Mother's.

Good night, with much love from your son,
Guy

After he healed from his battle injury, Howard returned to active duty, only to experience a year of humiliating battlefield defeats. A secret nickname for Howard was "Uh Oh," a play on O.O. Howard. In January 1863, Howard began attacking slavery with the fervor that he'd previously reserved for temperance. He wrote in a letter that appeared in the *New York Times*: "We must destroy slavery, root and branch.…This is a hard duty—a terrible, solemn duty; but it is a duty." In 1864, during the Atlanta Campaign, Howard redeemed himself and played a key role in Sherman's March to the Sea. Following the death of Major General James B. McPherson, Sherman favored Howard's leadership over that of John A. Logan, who was demoted. Later, when Sherman appealed to Howard, "as a Christian gentleman," to allow Logan to save face by riding at the head of the May 1865 Grand Review in Washington, D.C., Howard complied. General Sherman later called him a corps commander of "the utmost skill, nicety and precision."

At the war's end, in May 1865, Howard was asked to lead the Bureau of Refugees, Freedmen and Abandoned Lands; it was an agency that was supposed to provide humanitarian relief and usher people out of slavery and into their roles as citizens—right up Howard's alley. The cause of the freed people was Howard's new religion. But no government agency could produce the key to winning the hearts and minds of the Southerners who had been spurred on the quest for secession; for them, the war was hardly over. Howard had passion but lacked many of the skills he needed to navigate this leading role. Still, he believed education was "the true relief" from "beggary and dependence," and he poured his resources into that. But in the end, Howard's bureau folded, and he ended up accused of corruption. He was nearly wiped out by legal fees, but not before he was able to rally other socially conscious folks and the then-beseeched Congress to provide the funds to create Howard University. Founded in 1867, the coeducational school in Washington, D.C., was open to all races. Howard served as its president until 1874.

Howard was later acquitted on the charges of corruption and even got a vote of thanks for his efforts from the U.S. House of Representatives at the completion of the investigation. Howard was then ordered to Arizona to negotiate a peace treaty with the Chiricahua Apache leader Cochise to end to his decade-long war against American settlers. Howard secured a peace treaty by promising Cochise a reservation of his own choosing. Other generals thought the terms of this agreement were too generous, but, ultimately, almost the entire southeastern corner of Arizona was set aside as a Chiricahua reservation. Howard's success in this treaty and history's opinion of his time in the West is mixed. While things worked out for the Apache, it was a different story for the Nez Percé. He was able to negotiate with the tribe to get them to give up their homeland in the Wallowa Valley, but when he mentioned that they would be moved to a reservation that was assigned to them in Lapwai, Idaho, they disagreed, and Howard made it clear he would use force to move them if necessary.

After his time out West, Howard became the superintendent of West Point for several years, and he became the commanding officer of the Department of the Platte and the Division of the East. He finally retired from the army in 1894. Howard passed away suddenly of a heart attack on October 26, 1909. On the Saturday before his death, Howard had given a lecture in London, Ontario; the topic of the lecture was Abraham Lincoln. After his death, an honor guard from Fort Ethan Allen was placed at his home. His funeral was held the following Friday at Burlington's First Baptist Church.

12.

GOVERNOR URBAN WOODBURY

WHAT THE BISHOP SAW

The car was going like the devil. Please state that again; perhaps the court may not know just how fast that is.

The quote above was given by a witness named Edward Gillette in the court of Judge Mower as he testified in the case against Roy Buck, a chauffeur of Urban A. Woodbury, the entrepreneur, hotel owner and, apparently on the day his driver exceeded the downtown speed limits, a man on a mission.

The date of the hearing was September 28, 1910. The complaint against Buck had been made by James E. Burke, the former blacksmith who was also the city's Irish Catholic mayor. He was known as Burlington's "Progressive" mayor long before the name Bernie Sanders was even a whisper on the wind. Woodbury, himself, had been the first witness to testify, but he declined to take the stand. Instead, the former governor and hotelier positioned himself directly in front of the judge's desk, ignoring several hints from city attorney Mr. Vilas that the stand would be the more appropriate place for him to present his testimony. Woodbury remained in his spot in front of the judge as Gillette, a turnkey at the local jail, was called to the stand. When asked to give his version of the events, Gillette estimated the speed of the vehicle based on the speed of his horse that drove "ten miles per hour, sometimes." He continued, "I think I am going some then." The gallery broke into hysterics, and that's when Woodbury, in what might be seen as a highly irregular move today, attempted to question the witness himself. To be fair, Vilas objected, but Judge Mower offered that the ex-governor might be able to cross examine the witness later. It must have been hard to refuse Urban Woodbury, who, by the time the trial took place, was an extremely a high-profile and long-respected individual in the Burlington community.

Urban Adrain Woodbury was Vermont's first "empty sleeve"; he lost a limb during the Civil War and went right back into the fray. He was held prisoner and eventually attained the rank of captain in Company D of the Eleventh Regiment of Vermont volunteers. Before the war, Woodbury had graduated from UVM's medical school, but upon his return to Burlington, he abandoned medicine and took up the position as the general manager of the

Governor Urban Woodbury. *Photograph courtesy of the Library of Congress.*

lumber business that was owned by J.R. Booth. He held the position for nineteen years. He later married Paulina Darling of Elmore, Vermont, and, together, the couple had six children: Charles, Minnie, Gertrude, Edward, Lila and Mildred. Woodbury also became the principal owner of the Crystal Confectionery Company on College Street and was the president of the Queen City Cotton Company.

For more than thirty years, beginning in 1881, Woodbury was the owner and proprietor of the Van Ness Hotel on Main and St. Paul Streets. Bought in a foreclosure sale, the hotel's original frontage comprised about fifty feet before Woodbury expanded it with a western wing that took up another seventy-five feet of Main Street. He also added verandas, a ladies' parlor and other amenities. In 1900, a fire burned the hotel's stables, but Woodbury acquired more land on the western edge of the property and kept building. In 1904, he built an armory on the corner of Main and Pine Streets, next to his hotel, with space for the National Guard (his son was a captain of Company M) and meeting rooms for fraternal organizations like the Odd Fellows.

The Van Ness was one of the best-run and most popular hotels in the state, and Woodbury was proud of his staff. He always remarked that they were a part of the business's success, and he made a point to show his gratitude for their behavior by treating them "like human beings, giving

Van Ness House brochure. *Photograph courtesy of the University of Vermont, Special Collections.*

them care and sympathy when needed." He received their affection and respect in return; it was not uncommon for individuals to work for Woodbury for decades. On February 1, 1915, when Woodbury turned ownership of the hotel over to Max Powell and retired after thirty-four years, his staff gathered in the dining room to say their farewells and to present him with a handsome, gold-headed cane.

I'm not sure how he found the time, but Woodbury, a stalwart Republican, was also a Burlington alderman and, eventually, the mayor of the Queen City. He also went on to become the lieutenant governor and the governor of Vermont. He was a thirty-second-degree Mason, a Knight Templar and a member of the Mystic Shrine. He was also an Odd Fellow and the Knight of Pythias in the Grand Army of the Republic. Woodbury was also a member of the First Baptist Church of Burlington. He rubbed elbows with presidents, who visited him at his home (416 Pearl Street in Burlington) and his camp at Bluff Point in Colchester, Vermont. In 1898, President McKinley appointed Woodbury as the commissioner of the investigation into the conduct of the war with Spain; later, President Roosevelt appointed him as a member of the board of visitors at West Point. A commemorative bronze plaque, which was designed by the Woodbury's six children, was placed on their Pearl Street home in August 1936; it named three presidents who had been entertained there: McKinley, Roosevelt and Taft. During one of Roosevelt's visits to the Woodbury home, in 1902, the lights suddenly went out, causing the room full of dignitaries to fear that an attempt was being made on the president's life. Fortunately, it was just a power outage, but papers noted that Secret Service agents immediately moved to shield their commander in chief.

Urban Woodbury died on April 15, 1915. At his funeral, on April 18, 1915, four members of Vermont Company M guarded his solid mahogany casket, one at each corner. The casket was draped with the flag of the Loyal Legion and was topped with a cross of Easter lilies, an offering from Woodbury's six children. The casket was also topped with a wreath of galax, with glossy, heart-shaped leaves and small white flowers, from his nine grandchildren. Woodbury's honorary pallbearers included United States senators and congressmen, Vermont governors and prominent businessmen. Contingents from the Daughters of the American Revolution, the Sons of the American Revolution, the Society of Colonial Wars, the University of Vermont, several local manufacturing companies and Woodbury's former employees from the Hotel Van Ness and his other business ventures were also present. "Taps" was played, followed by Woodbury's favorite hymn, "Nearer My God to Thee."

On the cemetery's walking tours, visitors pass the spot where the Hotel Van Ness, which was lost to a fire in the 1950s, used to rise above Main Street and where the building that housed his confectionary company on College Street, now filled with apartments, still stands. On waterfront tours, guides tell the story of an astounding incident—a presumed UFO sighting—that Woodbury said he witnessed on July 2, 1907. The following is the story of the incident as it was recounted by Reverend Michaud in the *Monthly Weather Review*.

> *I was standing on the corner of Church and College Streets, just in front of the Howard Bank, and facing east, engaged in conversation with ex-Governor Woodbury and Mr. A.A. Buell, when, without the slightest indication or warning, we were startled by what sounded like a most unusual and terrific explosion, evidently very nearby. Raising my eyes and looking eastward along College Street, I observed a torpedo-shaped body, some three hundred feet away, stationary in appearance and suspended in the air, about fifty feet above the tops of buildings. In size, it was about six feet long by eight inches in diameter, the shell, having a dark appearance, with here and there tongues of fire issuing from spots on the surface, resembling red-hot, unburnished copper. Although stationary when first noticed, this object soon began to move, rather slowly, and disappeared over Dolan Brothers' store, southward. As it moved, the covering seemed rupturing in places, and through these, the intensely red flames issued.*

There were many witnesses to the event. W.P. Dodds said he saw the object from the window of his second-floor office at the Equitable Life Insurance Company on College Street. Merchants and citizens filled the street, trying to see what happened. A horse lay on the ground in front of the Standard Coal and Ice Company, and relieved onlookers watched as it rose to its feet. Witnesses claimed to see a ball of fire fly down and hit the torpedo-shaped object, and one said it hit the horse and bounced back into the sky. The *Burlington Free Press* and weather experts of the day quickly tried

Church and College Streets, circa early 1900s. *Photograph courtesy of the Library of Congress.*

to write the incident off as heat lightning and the witnesses as having too-fertile imaginations:

SAW BALL OF FIRE

ELECTRICAL DISTURBANCE THAT STARTLED BURLINGTONIANS YESTERDAY NOON

A forerunner to one of the heavy and frequent thunderstorms that have characterized the early summer in this vicinity startled Burlingtonians yesterday, just before noon. Without any preliminary disturbance of the atmosphere, there was a sharp report, the like of which is seldom heard. It was much louder in the business portion of the city than elsewhere, and particularly in the vicinity of Church and College Streets. People rushed to the street or to windows to learn what had happened, and when a horse was seen flat in the street in front of the Standard Coal and Ice Company's office, it was the general impression that the animal had been struck by lightning and killed. This theory was not long entertained, as the horse was soon struggling to regain his feet.

Ex-Governor Woodbury and Bishop Michaud were standing on the corner of Church and College Streets, in conversation, when the report startled them. In talking with a Free Press man later in the day, Governor Woodbury said his first thought was that an explosion had occurred somewhere in the immediate vicinity, and he turned, expecting to see bricks flying thru the air. Bishop Michaud was facing the east and saw a ball of fire rushing through the air, apparently just east of the National Biscuit Company's building. Alvaro Adsit also saw the ball of fire, as did a young man who was looking out of a window in the Strong Theater Building. Another man with a vivid imagination declared that the ball struck the center of College Street, near the Standard Coal and Ice Company's office, knocked the horse down by the jar [concussion] and then bounded up again to some undefined point in the sky.

So, by accident and by design, Urban Woodbury led an indisputably interesting life. But whatever happened to his speed-demon student chauffeur and the court case that was presided over by Judge Mower? The case was continued, but the author of this book can find no further mention of the incident. Perhaps Governor Woodbury, wielding his great influence, found a way to get the case dismissed. Or perhaps aliens erased all memory of the incident from the minds of Mayor Burke and Edward Gillette.

13.

LETTIE TRACY

IN-LAWS AND OUTLAWS

At Lakeview Cemetery, visitors will find a plot dedicated to the former residents of Burlington's Home for Aged Women. One such plot is that of Lettie (Irish) Tracy, who took her place at the home in 1935. At that time, the home was located at 272 Church Street, at a place that is known today as the Converse Home, a gracious assisted living and memory care community that is no longer just for ladies.

Lettie was born in Westford, Vermont, on July 14, 1862, to Lucius and Marilla (Cressey) Irish.

She later married a man from Essex, Vermont, named Hira B. Tracey. Tracy was described, when he was still a young boy, as "dull to a noticeable extent." Still, he had a "determined disposition," and when he set his mind to something, it was hard to change it. In addition to being stubborn, it seems that Hira also had a violent streak. When he was a married man, in his early twenties and still living on his family's farm, his father was gored to death by a bull. The bull was killed, but that didn't satisfy Hira; witnesses said he gouged the dead bull's eyes out and carried them away in his pockets.

In 1884, Lettie gave birth to the couple's daughter, Helen Marilla Tracy. At that time, Hira left farming, and the pair moved to Long Island, New York, but after a while, they returned to Burlington. They later moved back to New York, to New Rochelle, and while they were there, the pair ended up parting ways. Lettie, no longer willing to accept Hira's mistreatment, brought Helen back to Vermont. Hira took off to parts unknown; he was missing for sixteen years. In 1902, locals thought they'd found him. A man

The Converse home. *Photograph courtesy of Thea Lewis.*

came to town claiming that Hira Tracy was living out West under an alias; the man claimed that Hira was then *Harry* Tracy, a notorious outlaw. When she was approached by a journalist to get her take on the matter, Lettie burst into tears; she didn't want any part of the situation and realized that no good could come to her or her daughter from any association with Harry—or Hira.

Sometime later, it was discovered the outlaw in question was *not* her husband, whose extended family swore that he had never gotten farther west than Nebraska. Authorities had to admit that Hira's picture looked nothing like the bandit. The actual culprit was a man named Harry Severns, who was born on October 23, 1875. It's been supposed that, at one time, Tracy traveled with Butch Cassidy and his Hole in the Wall Gang. As an adult, Tracy committed numerous acts of robbery and violence. In March 1898, after a gunfight in Brown's Park, Colorado, in which a posse member was killed, Tracy was captured; but he escaped. In 1901, he was captured again, convicted and incarcerated at the Oregon State Penitentiary. He broke out of that jail as well, with an accomplice named David Merrill; the pair killed three corrections officers in their getaway. They were on the lam for a month, when, after they were most likely getting on each other's nerves, they argued and decided to duel it out. Tracy cheated and spun around early, killing Merrill.

On July 3, 1902, Tracy set up an ambush near Bothell, Washington, where he killed two law enforcement officials and fled, taking several hostages. This heist ended in another shootout. He ultimately committed suicide to avoid capture on August 6, 1902. The *Seattle Times* wrote: "In all the criminal lore of the country, there is no record equal to that of Harry Tracy for cold-blooded nerve, desperation and thirst for crime. Jesse James, compared with Tracy, is a Sunday school teacher."

Whether Hira was a killer or not, Lettie Tracy was probably better off without her wandering ex. She later sued him for desertion and "intolerable severity," and she was granted a divorce in May 1905. Lettie kept herself busy as a member of Burlington's First Baptist Church, and the community gossip section of the *Burlington Free Press* reported her many visits to her family members and friends who lived in St. Albans, Cambridge and Jericho, Vermont. She even completed several trips to Vermont while she was living in Sanborn, Florida, where her daughter had made a home for her. After returning to Vermont, Lettie lived for a year with her friend, Mrs. L.M. Jordan of Jericho, before moving to Burlington's Home for Aged Women on April 11, 1935.

The home had existed in several locations before it moved to 272 Church Street around 1922. It was once located on the corner of Bank and St. Paul Streets, in what was then one of the oldest buildings in the city. The building, which has since been torn down, was erected by Sion Howard, the sibling of philanthropists John P. and Louisa Howard. It was a designed with a view of the lake in mind and featured many western-facing windows, a cupola at the top and large common rooms. It was decorated with stained-glass accents over its front door and in its dining room. The new home was originally built in 1799 by William Chase Harrington, one of Burlington's earliest attorneys. Harrington was a prosecutor in the trail of Cyrus P. Dean, an Irishman who, as part of an eight-man smuggling

Original sign from the Home for Aged Women. *Photograph courtesy of the Converse Home.*

party on the ship *Black Snake*, had the murder of a farmer named John Ormsby pinned on him. Dean was executed in Burlington, at a site close to what is now Elmwood Cemetery.

When Harrington owned the home, it was surrounded by an eighty-acre farm, which included an orchard and sugar woods—quite a difference from the busy family neighborhood near Burlington's downtown that it is today. The home had previously passed through the hands of multiple owners, including the Reverend John K. Converse, who established the Burlington Female Sanctuary there. On July 23, 1936, a little more than a year after Lettie moved into the home, she received a special birthday gift. Blanche Ring, a "stage and screen star" who was in town performing at the Green Mountain Playhouse, visited the aged women to sing a "program of old songs" in honor of ladies whose birthdays occurred in July.

Like the Converse Home is today, the Home for Aged Women had no shortage of interesting social activities. This author's particular favorite was the Halloween Supper, an event during which the rooms were decorated in "pumpkin colors," with lanterns and candles all around. Before the ladies were seated, they were each given a little red or yellow cap, which they wore for the duration of the festivities. Afterward, they gathered in the drawing room for a group photo. It's nice to know that Lettie Tracy passed her final days in a home filled with so much care and concern. She passed away on Tuesday, December 3, 1940. The following Friday, before her interment at Lakeview Cemetery, a service of remembrance was held at the home.

14.

JOHN LYONS

BUFFALO SOLDIER

John R. Lyons came to Vermont in July 1909, as a Buffalo soldier, ready to serve a four-year stint at Fort Ethan Allen in Colchester. He was young, just twenty-one years old, and Vermont was a different world. Buffalo soldiers were African American soldiers who served on the western frontier after the American Civil War. In 1866, six all-black cavalry and infantry regiments were created after Congress passed the Army Organization Act. The Buffalo soldiers' main tasks were to help control the Native Americans of the plains, to capture cattle rustlers and thieves and to protect settlers, stagecoaches, wagon trains and railroad crews along the western front.

No one knows for certain why, but the soldiers of the all-black Ninth and Tenth Cavalry Regiments were dubbed "buffalo soldiers" by the Native Americans they encountered. One theory claims that the nickname arose because the soldiers' dark, curly hair resembled the fur of buffalo. Another assumption is that the soldiers fought so fiercely that the Native Americans revered them and said they were as strong as the mighty plains buffalo. Whatever the reason, the name stuck.

Buffalo soldiers bolstered America's westward movement, protecting settlers as towns sprang up and communities formed. They also protected the nation's amenities, like roads, railroad lines and mail delivery lines, that stretched the fingers of progress across the continent. They built and renovated dozens of posts and strung thousands of miles of telegraph wire. They opened new roads and mapped thousands of miles of uncharted country. The Buffalo soldiers were involved in dozens battles

A winding path at Lakeview Cemetery. *Photograph courtesy of Thea Lewis.*

with the Native Americans, including the Red River War against the Kiowas, Comanches, Cheyenne and the Arapahoe. There were also skirmishes between the Buffalo soldiers and the Mescalero Apaches in what is now Guadalupe Mountains National Park, and the Buffalo soldiers were involved in a slew of bloody conflicts with native settlers on both sides of the United States-Mexican border. These skirmishes broke out after a Warm Springs Apache named Victorio fled the reservation in southeastern New Mexico with a number of his followers in 1879. The buffalo soldiers also fought in the Spanish-American War, traveling to Cuba and the Philippines.

But when the Buffalo soldiers arrived in Vermont, they realized that it was a different deal altogether. Their first fall and winter in Vermont found them still wearing the uniforms that had been issued to them in the summer; they were completely unprepared for the sometimes blistering cold that their new post had to offer. Inspections and guard tours were carried out in biting winds and, sometimes, full blizzards, which made the Buffalo soldiers' transitions into their new lives more difficult. While the weather was cold, so, for a time, was the reception from some of the locals.

Today, Vermont has a reputation for being one of the whitest states in the nation. When the buffalo soldiers made their way into the Green Mountain State, it was even less diverse. The Tenth Cavalry, which numbered about 1,500 men, arrived to find a community of about 25,000 in which not everyone was happy to see them. The introduction of a significant number of "colored" soldiers to the area disturbed and dismayed many residents. This feeling was, unfortunately, fueled by the local newspapers, the *Burlington Free Press* and the *Rutland Herald*, which initially promoted the narrative that these black soldiers were lawless and destructive.

The initial response from some citizens was to keep the troops segregated from the general populace, but the idea didn't catch fire. A reason for this may have been the basic integrity of most Vermonters, and the opinions of people with influence, like Elias Lyman, who owned the local coal company and was president of the Burlington Traction Company. When it was suggested that the trolleys be segregated, Lyman wouldn't stand for it and said that it wouldn't happen on his watch. Negative press regarding segregation, by papers like the *New York Times*, also played a part in the acceptance of the soldiers by the general population. The Times called Vermonters' concerns "foolish, and … unpatriotic and unworthy." The *Boston Traveler* wrote that Vermonters were acting "not unlike their southern brethren."

With few exceptions, the troops proved to be a positive addition to the Burlington community. Many brought their wives and children to live in the area, and, instead of seeing color, townspeople saw families. Eventually, the citizens of Vermont and the local papers praised the soldiers for their gentlemanly conduct. The Buffalo soldiers also brought an element of entertainment to Vermont that had largely been missing. Some of the men played baseball and basketball on a level that had never been seen locally. So many residents turned out to watch their competitions that the pastors and chaplains of local religious organizations requested the soldiers' commanding officer to stop the summer baseball games, which were keeping parishioners from attending services. The commander let the clergymen know that the games would continue. "This is Sunday," he told them, "and we don't tell our troopers what to do on Sunday."

It's unclear whether John Ralph Lyons was one of the soldiers who brought spectators to their feet during sporting events, but we do know that he was born February 22, 1888, in Lewistown, Mifflin County, Pennsylvania, the grandson of a runaway slave named Benjamin Lyons, who settled in Salemville, Pennsylvania, around 1825. John's parents were James Levi Lyons, a barber and musician, and Harriet (Baptist) Lyons. Together, the couple had six children, four boys and two girls. Harriet died in childbirth when John was just a teenager.

He served in the 10th Cavalry, Troop D, for six years; he spent the last four years of his service at Fort Ethan Allen. On July 6, 1911, he was awarded the Silver Lifesaving Medal "for bravely rescuing a companion" at Mallets Bay in Colchester, Vermont. He was discharged from the army in 1914 but rejoined in 1917, enlisting in Company F of the 807th Pioneer Infantry. After serving overseas during World War I, he returned to Vermont and worked as a civilian barber at Fort Ethan Allen. Later in his life, John worked at the American Woolen Mills in Winooski.

John Lyons was light-skinned, and it has been written that, at the time he met his wife, an Irish immigrant from Dover, New Hampshire, named Elizabeth Connell, he was "passing for white." He and Lizzie (as she was called) were married in 1918. Together, they raised six daughters and two sons in Winooski and Burlington, Vermont. Lyons's home life was not without its ups and downs; the *Burlington Free Press* chronicles his arrests for domestic disputes, including one incident in which, during a disagreement with two of his daughters, he chased them down the street with a meat cleaver. On March 16, 1941, while Lyons was hauling coal, working at the American Woolen Mills in Winooski, he was kicked in the chest by a mule. He died at home later that day.

15.

ALVARO ADSIT

BURLINGTON'S FIRST PHONE EXCHANGE

How much do you pay a year for your telephone service? In Burlington in 1921, subscribers to the telephone exchange, which was started by Alvaro Adsit and his partner, Dr. Walter S. Vincent, paid a base price of $20.00—$259.00 in today's money. There was also a toll, or what people today would call a long-distance rate, at the time; an additional $0.10 was added to call Colonel Greenleaf's drugstore in Winooski, on the corner of Main and East Allen Streets.

Alvaro Adsit was born on March 26, 1849, in Chesterfield, New York, to Hollis and Mary (Bigelow) Adsit. He traveled to Burlington as a young man and lived in the Queen City for many decades—long enough to be deemed, upon his death, "one of the city's oldest businessmen." He gained a reputation for being an entrepreneur, merchant, photographer, sailor and, apparently, the genius who conceptualized what was said to be the world's third telephone exchange. He did the latter from behind a desk in the offices of his Queen City coal business, Adsit and Bigelow.

In papers he typed up for his son, Robert J. Adsit, a few years before his death, he revealed his fascination for Alexander Graham Bell's invention.

I had read several good magazine articles describing it and bought a couple of cheap instruments made of wood, then I made two more and installed a line between the coal office and the coal yard. The line worked, but not satisfactorily. The telephone was considered, at that time, merely a scientific toy, and the transmitter and exchange systems had not been developed.

He went on to describe his partnership with Vincent, who had been contacted by Theodore Vail of the new Bell Telephone Company. Vail had come to Burlington with an "old black bag" full of phones, hoping to entice someone into starting an exchange with their equipment for a reduced rental fee of five dollars per piece, per year. Vincent had no technical experience but worked out a partnership with Adsit in what became the Burlington Telephone Exchange.

The exchange's list of subscribers in 1880 numbered around 160. During this time, as they are with modern cell phones, the receiver and transmitter were combined on one piece of equipment.

Alvaro Adsit portrait. *Photograph courtesy of the University of Vermont, Special Collections.*

Unfortunately, unlike today's phones, the technology was new and often wonky, so the exchange wrote instructions on the introductory page of the its new directory:

> *Remember that a distinct articulation in an ordinary or a low tone of voice is more easily heard than a rapid speech in a high key.*
>
> *If you have but one instrument, after speaking, transfer the telephone from mouth to ear very promptly.*
>
> *When replying to a communication from another, do not speak too quickly. Be sure that your correspondent has finished speaking, and give him time to transfer, as much of the trouble is noticed daily from both parties speaking at the same time.*
>
> *In using the transmitter, speak about eight to twelve inches from the instrument, and do not raise the voice when asked to repeat a message. This rule will save much daily embarrassment and valuable time, as our older patrons are often observed to disregard it.*

All told, the partners invested $634 into the project. After three years, they sold the exchange to Bell Telephone for a net profit of $27,766. Bell Telephone asked if they wanted the funds in cash or stocks; the pair laughed—what would they want with a bunch of Bell stock? Adsit said that the only time he'd ever felt rich was when he got the payout for his half of the deal, but he

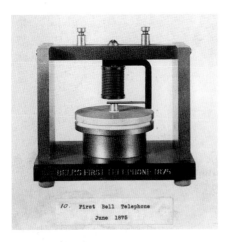

10. First Bell Telephone
June 1875

Alexander Graham Bell's first telephone.
Photograph courtesy of the Library of Congress.

wrote sometime later, "A few years ago, one of the Boston papers had an article showing how, if a person invested in Bell Telephone about the time we started in, when the stock was very low, and the amount issued comparatively small, and had left it in, it would be worth a $1 million." Naturally, the descendants of Adsit who were interviewed for this book wish that the men had taken the stock option.

In addition to his coal and telephone enterprises, Adsit had a grocery business on the corner of College and Mechanic Streets, and with his partner, W.F. Ferguson, he ran another College Street business that manufactured saddle hardware. With his fingers in so many of Burlington's commercial pies, Adsit was bound to be tending at least one of his businesses during the presumed UFO sighting that occurred in the middle of the Queen City in the summer of 1907. The following is his eyewitness account of the incident.

> *I was standing in my store* [Ferguson and Adsit's Store], *facing the north. My attention was attracted by this, "ball of fire" apparently descending toward a point on the opposite side of the street in front of the Hall Furniture Store, when, within 18 or 20 feet of the ground, the ball exploded with a deafening sound. The ball, before the explosion, was apparently 8 or 10 inches in diameter. The halo of light resulting from the explosion was 8 to 10 feet in diameter, the light had a yellowish tinge, somewhat like candlelight; no noise or sound was heard before the explosion; no damage was done so far as is known to me.*

Many historical references to Adsit include the title commodore, as he logged many hours near and on the lake, building and racing sailboats for fun. Adsit enjoyed spending time at his second home on Thompson's Point in Charlotte, Vermont, with his family; his wife, Josephine (Lanou); and their children, Robert and Margery. Adsit selected property after deciding it had "the best wind." A familiar sight on his large sailboat, *Sandalon*, Adsit

Alvaro Adsit's photography. *Photograph courtesy of the University of Vermont, Special Collections.*

The Alvaro Adsit monument. *Photograph courtesy of Thea Lewis.*

was also on the executive committee of the Lake Champlain Yacht Club. He had a keen eye for photography, and he entered and won a number of competitions, as listed in the *Photographic Times*. Adsit was also a city alderman and served on several city boards.

He died after a "two-year" illness on March 27, 1923, the day after his seventy-fourth birthday, at his home at 394 Pearl Street. The location is now the site of UVM's Jeanne Mance Hall and was once part of the old Trinity College campus.

16

ELIHU B. TAFT

GOOD INTENTIONS

When Elihu B. Taft died, he gave the city of Burlington a choice: He'd donate his estate, which was located at the corner of Pearl and Williams Street, to be the location of either a schoolhouse or a courthouse. If the city decided to build neither, the funds would go to build a home for aged men. If the structure they did build ceased to be used for its intended purpose, it would then be designated as a shelter for older homeless men. When people don't follow the rules, lawsuits often follow, and this situation was a case in point. But the town couldn't blame Taft; the lawyer, who was later known as Judge Taft, was a smart, conscientious fellow who thought he had his post-mortem ducks in a row.

Born in Williston, Vermont, to Eleazer T. Taft and Ellen M. Barber on March 25, 1847, Taft was always a stand-up guy. He attended the University of Vermont, was a member of the Lambda Iota Fraternity and graduated with the class of 1871. Instead of attending law school, Taft clerked for the bar—something that was pretty common back in the day—with Wales & Taft and was admitted to the bar in 1873. Throughout his career, Taft handled many estates and trusts—all with the utmost discretion—and he always treated his clients' assets and concerns in the same way that he would treat his own. On April 1, 1875, he married Lucia Johnson, who died the following December. He never remarried.

In Burlington, he was a city alderman for thirteen years and a state senator for two. He was also a register of the probate court and served for a few months as the acting judge of the probate court—just long enough, it seems, to be permanently be recognized by the title. He lived simply but traveled extensively in the United States and beyond. In his lifetime, he was able to visit Europe, Mexico, India and Egypt. He was considered a warm, good-hearted man, with the courage of his convictions. He was a "lover of sobriety" and a defender of justice. He had a reputation for not sticking his nose into the business of others; yet, he wasn't afraid to express his opinion when asked, even if it wasn't popular. Judge Taft was a voracious reader and was interested in a wide range of topics. He was religious and attended the Unitarian church faithfully until he was too ill and feeble to go.

He was a nature lover, and he didn't mind getting his hands dirty. It was noted he loved "all shy and growing things." The natural, "old-fashioned" garden he tended at his Pearl Street home was called one of the Queen City's "summer glories." He loved to test new plant specimens and particularly loved watching the birds they attracted. He was a member of the Botany Club of Vermont, the Bird Club of Vermont, the Sierra Club and the Green Mountain Club. As one of his last public acts, he arranged for a shelter to be built "on the chin" of Mount Mansfield for travelers hiking Vermont's Long Trail. The *Burlington Free Press* ended his obituary, which was printed on January 14, 1929, with a fitting poem.

Hollyhocks tall and maiden white lilies,
When next you peep from your mantles of green,
You shall not find him in paths of the morning.
He has passed off in the sunset serene.
High brooding elms and whispering larches,
Martens and robins and orioles of spring,
Vain is your calling, your piping and whistling,
Yet the soul of him lists to the music you bring.

As for the bequest of his estate to Burlington, he envisioned a "plain and substantial" brick building "trimmed with Barre granite," no more than two stories tall and, alas, no belfry, since the available funds probably wouldn't allow for it. He did specify that he'd like for the building, whatever it was, to be named after him.

The city purchased a piece of property adjacent Judge Taft's that had previously been owned by Mary L. Saunders, and the Elihu B. Taft School was built there in 1938. It served the community as an elementary school for forty-two years but was closed in 1980, due to a shortage of young children in the neighborhood. The Burlington School Department used the school

A postcard depicting the Elihu Taft Elementary School. *Photograph courtesy of Thea Lewis.*

building for administrative offices until 1985, when it leased space to the hospital and a few other organizations.

Some citizens, who cited Judge Taft's intentions as they were stated in his will, objected to these developments. In 1986, a lawsuit was filed, and demonstrations, protests, and sit-ins by groups like the Homeless Empowerment Coalition ensued. In 1987, a judge ruled that the building could continue to be leased to non-school entities. However, the judge placed a time limit on his ruling: five years. Sometime later, Roger Wilder, a member of the Homeless Empowerment Coalition, called the way that the court had allowed the changes "weasel-worded" (a term that this author hopes they have the opportunity to employ at some future date). Wilder thought it would be fairer for the homeless to benefit, either by sharing the space or by sharing in the proceeds from the rent.

In 1995, just as the school district, which was then led by Superintendent Donna Jemilo, hoped to sell the building and apply the money elsewhere, a codicil was discovered in Taft's will. City attorney Joe McNeil stated the opinion that the codicil, which had not been filed with probate, negated the original intent of Taft's will and the need for the building to be converted into a shelter for indigent or aged men. One advocate for the homeless said that McNeil was "trying to circumvent the real intentions of a very honorable man."

The controversy dragged on until 2013, when it was announced that UVM, which wanted to include the property in its campus master plan, was going to *rent* the building—not purchase it—for eighty years at a rate of $20,000 per year. The university also paid the rent up-front and had the option to rent for another eighty years at the rate of $1 per year. The university also covered the building's operating costs, which came out to around $70,000 per year. It was a nice little workaround. In the end, Chittenden superior court judge Susan Fowler ruled that the lease was consistent with Taft's will, as UVM would use the building for educational purposes. The city council voted to approve the plan.

But this was not the end of the controversies associated with Elihu Taft's namesake. On October 16, 1946, thirty-two sixth-grade students from Elihu Taft Elementary traveled to meet the famed American artist and transplanted Vermonter Norman Rockwell. Rockwell, who was fifty-two years old at the time, had invited the group to his studio in Arlington, Vermont. Among the sixth graders was a bright-eyed eleven-year-old named Alison Pooley. Alison was popular with the other kids and was a child who would later be described by her former classmate as "a marvelous person." When the group arrived, Rockwell showed them how he created his paintings, including his now-iconic *Saturday Evening Post* covers. He later signed autographs and gave them apples from his own orchard. Alison, who was the daughter of a University of Vermont classics professor and a homemaker, enjoyed every minute of the trip, but that was only natural. According to her family and friends, Alison was a bright, bubbly, outgoing kid who loved life and new adventures. She was well-rounded, confident and a lot of fun. She never shied from chatting with strangers. People called her "special."

Unfortunately, during the very next summer, while at camp, Alison took ill. It was discovered that she had leukemia, and she died on September 11, right after the start of the new school year. Her devastated classmates, in the hopes that Norman Rockwell would create a fitting painting as a way to remember her, raised $48 to pay the artist. What he gave them was the now-timeless portrait called *Babysitter with Screaming Infant*, or the *Babysitter* for the purposes of this book. The painting depicts a little girl having a very unpleasant experience caring for a screaming infant who's got a firm grip on her pigtail. (The painting came with an actual safety pin poked through the canvas where a diaper lays across a chair.) Rockwell declined their payment, so the class used the $48 to buy a plaque in Alison's honor.

In 1978, before the Burlington School Department closed Taft Elementary to students, the painting was appraised and valued at $30,000. It was held for safekeeping by the now-defunct Chittenden Bank and was forgotten until 1995, when the school district, which was short on cash, started going through its administrative couch cushions and digging out its assets. When it inquired about the painting's value, it learned that the painting was worth a lot more than $30,000—in fact, it was worth ten times as much. The school board began mulling over selling the painting in order to bolster their sagging coffers, and the local paper announced the sale. Two Pooley classmates, a former UVM employee named Lynne Swan and David Jenkins, a superior court judge, called the sale a halt. The pair was joined by a Rockwell model and Arlington neighbor named James Edgerton. The men maintained that the *Babysitter* was not the school department's painting to do with as it wished; they claimed that the painting belonged to Alison Pooley's classmates.

In 2015, Samuel Bloomberg, a Burlington lawyer came up with a solution and suggested the formation of what became the Save the Babysitter campaign, which raised funds equivalent to the painting's value in order to save it from sale. Consequently, the *Babysitter* is still in the Burlington School Department's collection. At its last appraisal, the twenty-six-by-twenty-eight-inch painting was valued at $900,000. Today, it can be seen at the Robert Hull Fleming Museum on the UVM campus.

17

H.O. WHEELER

A SUPERIOR SUPERINTENDENT OF SCHOOLS

Henry Orson Wheeler was born in Williston, Vermont, on October 7, 1841, the son of son of Reverend Orville Gould Wheeler, a South Hero school principal, and his wife, Aurelia (Sanford). When the call came for men to enlist in the army during the Civil War, Wheeler left his studies at the University of Vermont and enlisted on the buddy system with his friend Zebina Landon of South Hero, Vermont. Both men joined the First Cavalry, Company A, but Wheeler outlived Landon, who died as a prisoner on August 22, 1862, in Richmond, Virginia, at the age of twenty-four.

Wheeler survived the war, but he didn't have an easy ride. It was reported that he was killed at the Battle of Hagerstown, but he had, instead, eluded the enemy and tended to another soldier named Homer Bliss, who later died from his injuries. On a failed maneuver to capture Mobile, Alabama, known as Bank's Retreat, Wheeler was captured and separated from his company. He eventually escaped, wandering for several days before he managed to rejoin his regiment. Fortunately, his horse and bags had been recovered.

Later, Wheeler was wounded at the Battle of the Wilderness, on the first day of General Grant's advance; he was shot through the lungs. After the battle, he was transported back to Vermont, but, while he was still injured, Wheeler returned to battle under General Philip Henry Sheridan, a man who was once described by Abraham Lincoln as "a brown, chunky little chap, with a long body, short legs, not enough neck to hang him." Nevertheless, Sheridan was immortalized in a poem by Thomas Buchanan Read. Titled "Sheridan's Ride," the poem is one that glorifies Sheridan's ability to turn disaster into victory during one of the most dramatic rides in United States history. It's a beautiful poem, and it's easy to see why Sheridan was pleased with it.

Up from the South, at break of day,
Bringing to Winchester fresh dismay,
The affrighted air with a shudder bore,
Like a herald in haste to the chieftain's door,
The terrible grumble, and rumble, and roar,
Telling the battle was on once more,
And Sheridan twenty miles away.
And wider still those billows of war
Thundered along the horizon's bar;
And louder yet into Winchester rolled
The roar of that red sea uncontrolled,
Making the blood of the listener cold,
As he thought of the stake in that fiery fray,
With Sheridan twenty miles away.
But there is a road from Winchester town,
A good, broad highway leading down:
And there, through the flush of the morning light,
A steed as black as the steeds of night
Was seen to pass, as with eagle flight;
As if he knew the terrible need,
He stretched away with his utmost speed.
Hills rose and fell, but his heart was gay,
With Sheridan fifteen miles away.
Still sprang from those swift hoofs, thundering south,
The dust like smoke from the cannon's mouth,
Or the trail of a comet, sweeping faster and faster,
Foreboding to traitors the doom of disaster.
The heart of the steed and the heart of the master
Were beating like prisoners assaulting their walls,
Impatient to be where the battle-field calls;
Every nerve of the charger was strained to full play,
With Sheridan only ten miles away.
Under his spurning feet, the road
Like an arrowy Alpine river flowed,
And the landscape sped away behind

Like an ocean flying before the wind;
And the steed, like a barque fed with furnace ire,
Swept on, with his wild eye full of fire;
But, lo! he is nearing his heart's desire;
He is snuffing the smoke of the roaring fray,
With Sheridan only five miles away.
The first that the general saw were the groups
Of stragglers, and then the retreating troops;
What was to be done? what to do?—a glance told him both.
Then striking his spurs with a terrible oath,
He dashed down the line, 'mid a storm of huzzas,
And the wave of retreat checked its course there, because
The sight of the master compelled it to pause.
With foam and with dust the black charger was gray;
By the flash of his eye, and his red nostril's play,
He seemed to the whole great army to say:
"I have brought you Sheridan all the way
From Winchester down to save the day."
Hurrah! hurrah for Sheridan!
Hurrah! hurrah for horse and man!
And when their statues are placed on high
Under the dome of the Union sky,
The American soldier's Temple of Fame,
There, with the glorious general's name,
Be it said, in letters both bold and bright:
"Here is the steed that saved the day
By carrying Sheridan into the fight,
From Winchester—twenty miles away!"

Under Sheridan, Wheeler was taken prisoner. The Rebel faction threatened his life and took all of his clothes, leaving him in his underwear. He was marched for several days without food and was eventually locked up in Libby Prison in Richmond, Virginia. Libby Prison, which was originally built as a food warehouse, was infamous for its harsh conditions. It was overcrowded in the extreme sense of the word. At one point, one thousand prisoners were stuffed into two cavernous rooms that had open, barred windows, which exposed the to the elements—both freezing and stifling. Diseases ran rampant through the prison population, and many suffered from malnutrition. A large number of Libby's prisoners died while incarcerated there. But fortunately for Wheeler, while he was being instructed to strip off his clothes, he was resourceful enough to slip fifty dollars down his pants without being noticed. He used the money for payoffs, and it made the time he spent incarcerated much easier to endure. He was released through the prisoner exchange and parole program and was promoted to brevet captain on March 13, 1865; he mustered out later that year.

Once Wheeler was back in Vermont, he resumed his studies at the university, graduating in 1867. He went on to study law at the University of Michigan in Ann Arbor and passed the bar exam in June 1868. He first worked with a firm in Janesville, Wisconsin. In 1869, he moved to Iowa, where he was admitted to the bar, but a few years later, he returned to his home state to practice law in Burlington.

He eventually married Elizabeth Lavina Martin, and, together, they had five sons; two of them, Henry O. Wheeler and S. Harley Wheeler, became military men. Orville Gould Wheeler was so bright that he graduated from high school a year early, in 1934, and took a "gap year" to work for the *Burlington Free Press* as a clerk in its stationery store. After he graduated from UVM, Orville became a book publisher. Edward eventually left Vermont

H.O. Wheeler monument. *Photograph courtesy of Thea Lewis.*

and traveled to San Dimas, California, where he became manager of a local orange grower's association. John Wheeler became an eminent eye specialist and once saved the sight of the king of Siam.

H.O. Wheeler served on the Burlington School Board for several years, and in 1880, he was elected as the superintendent of the Burlington schools, a position he held for over thirty years. During his tenure as superintendent, H.O. also served a ten-year term as the treasurer of the University of Vermont. H.O. was all about progress; during his thirty-two-year tenure leading the Burlington school system, eight schools were built within the city's limits. His namesake, H.O. Wheeler School, was built in 1904 on Burlington's Archibald Street, and it is now known as the Integrated Arts Academy. After retiring from his position as the superintendent of schools, H.O. and his wife, Elizabeth, relocated. They had enjoyed visits with their son Edward in San Dimas and decided to make it their permanent home.

When H.O. Wheeler passed on July 17, 1918, at the home of his son Edward, in San Dimas, California, he'd been ill for some time. After her husband's death, Elizabeth returned to Vermont every year and spent her summers at a cabin that she and her husband had owned on Cedar Beach, in Charlotte, Vermont. It was a trip she made regularly until a few years before her death. Elizabeth died in Los Angeles, California, at the home of her son H.O. Wheeler Jr., on June 29, 1934, and she was interred near her husband in Lakeview Cemetery.

18

PHILOMENE LEMOINE

CALL HER MADAME

No person shall keep a house of prostitution or suffer or permit any prostitution in any house or building he or she may occupy, or be an inmate in any house of ill fame, or in any manner contribute to the support or maintenance of any house of ill fame, nor shall any person having control of any house or building, lease or rent the same to any prostitute or prostitutes to be kept as a house of ill fame.
—*Burlington City Ordinances, chapter XXVI, section 4*

When it came to certain city ordinances, Philomene Pasha Cathey, whose aliases included Philomene Lemoine and Philomene Deo, thought that they were made to be broken. She broke them regularly in her great big bordello at 38 Intervale Avenue in Burlington, and she was constantly raided by Burlington's police department. Philomene Lemoine was Burlington's most notorious madame; she was a dame who never flew under the radar. Her "house of ill fame," as brothels were called in late 1800s and early 1900s, was infamous in Burlington even before 1883, when she built the large Queen Anne home with Colonial elements that she lived in until her death.

Philomene was born in Burlington in November 1835, to Joseph and Louisa (Gaboree) Pasha, who had immigrated to Burlington from the province of Quebec. Little is known about her father, but her mother lived an extraordinarily long life and managed to stay interested and useful until the age of 105. Despite a hip fracture at the age of 91, Philomene's mother moved about with the aid of a chair, and she even participated in some household tasks until the last few weeks of her life, before her death in January 1906.

Philomene grew up on Battery Street and eventually married Jerry Deo, who owned a saloon on Church Street. The records of their union are scant, and Philomene never used his name professionally. She was, early on, known by her maiden name, Philomene Pasha, but she mostly went by the surname Lemoine. Even in the later years of her "career," after her marriage to George T. Cathey, the town's papers still referenced her famous alias. Philomene had two children: a daughter, Nina, who lived to adulthood and married a man named Joseph Bacon, and Isadore, who predeceased her. It is unclear, but assumed, that they were both the children of Jerry Deo. The only occupation that was ever listed for Philomene was "housewife," a title that barely covers her responsibilities at 38 Intervale Avenue.

Time and time again, Philomene was hauled to the courthouse. Most of the time, she was brought in for the simple—if you can call it that— act of aiding in prostitution and running a house of "ill-fame," but other times, she was brought in for scuffles that broke out in her place. There were a few times that she was brought to the courthouse for what appeared to be harboring girls from other countries, who the authorities and newspaper reporters referred to as "immoral aliens." When the authorities weren't nabbing her for her usual infractions, they were trying to catch her conducting other illegal activities. The May 29, 1901 issue of the *Burlington Free Press* stated, "Sheriff Thomas Reeves and Turnkey Charles Quinn searched the premises of Mrs. Philomene Cathey, better known as Philomene Lemoine, yesterday morning but found no intoxicating liquor. Several bottles of soft drinks were found."

Philomene's home at 38 Intervale Avenue was the perfect location for making a living at, what author Rudyard Kipling called "the most ancient profession in the world." It was a five-minute walk to her place from Burlington's busy downtown, and the home was only a block from the North Street business district. Considering the sums she paid in bail money, Philomene's business must have been good. Sometimes, eleven or twelve women, were rounded up from her place in one night. She was fined, fined again and fined some more. It didn't seem to deter her. Records show that she was pinched for aiding and abetting the flesh trade from the 1870s to the early 1900s—a good, long stretch.

Later in life, she married George T. Cathey, a much younger man, who was not one to keep a low profile. His profession was listed as "construction," but he seemed to have a lot of free time for a construction worker. He racked up assaults; was sued by a woman for losing control of his automobile and splashing her and her carriage with mud and household refuse from a ditch on the side the road; and he couldn't even keep track of his dog. The October 3, 1908 edition of the *Burlington Free Press* stated, "Setter dog lost, color white and lemon, no collar, answers to name of Buck. Liberal reward will be paid for return to George Cathey, 38 Intervale Avenue."

In October 1909, things began to wind down for Philomene. The city attorney wanted outlaws and the community at large to know that the city and its local law enforcement meant business. An October 2, 1909 article in the *Burlington Free Press* read:

> *Copies of the ordinance, "to suppress immoral practices in the city of Burlington" have been furnished by city attorney Martin S. Vilas to each of the regular policemen with instructions to report violations of the same to the chief of police when, upon confident evidence prosecutions, would ensue. Sheriff Allen and his deputies have given aid to the work in the recent raid of the place at 38 Intervale Avenue, upon warrants issued by the city attorney for violations of this ordinance. Eleven prosecutions and convictions in city court resulted from this raid. The keeper of this place, Mrs. Philomene Lamoine, was notified in court by the city attorney that she must close this place and stop her illegal business, or he would drive her out by repeated prosecutions. The departments of the sheriff and the police report that the nine girls convicted in court have all left town and that the proprieties, for the first time in very many years, has closed her place.*
>
> *Other raids on places of similar character but lesser notoriety are likely soon to be made.*

Lemoine also owned some property on the southeast corner of Battery and Main Streets that was known as the Russell House. It was a hotel that was also famous for its sexual shenanigans, some involving girls as young as seventeen. Philomene and George Cathey sold the Russell House in 1910. At this time, Philomene was in her seventies, she'd lost her mother several years before and her health wasn't what it had been. Winding down probably seemed like a good plan to her. Her name is notably absent from the pages of the local newspaper in the years before she passed, and it was noted in her death notice that the poor of Burlington would miss her—perhaps she turned her energies toward philanthropy.

Philomene Pasha Cathey died on January 10, 1914 at the age of seventy-eight. Her death certificate lists her cause of death as diabetes mellitus, with the contributing factor of "general debility," or plain old age. In the end, Philomene was still married to George Cathey, who was living in Asheville, North Carolina at the time of her death. A quick sweep of the internet shows that a man with the same name was killed in the Langren Hotel in Asheville on Valentine's Day 1921; the forty-eight-year-old man was shot five times in the head with a pistol. The murder was never investigated.

Philomene Pasha Cathey's funeral was held at her home at 38 Intervale Avenue at 2:00 p.m. Her body was placed in the vault at Lakeview Cemetery to await interment at a later, warmer date. Her will stipulated that she be buried beside her son.

19

LUELLA WHEELER

A STAR-SPANGLED HEART

Luella Wheeler, ANC (Army Nurse Corps), was born on May 7, 1883, to Hemen Holmes Wheeler, a dairy farmer from Fairfax, Vermont, and his wife, Alice Cornelia (Smith) of Shelburne. Luella was one of six children and grew up in what was then rural South Burlington, Vermont. In 1900, the United States Federal Census records show that the ages of the children in the Wheeler home spanned from two to twenty. The household included Luella's maternal grandmother, Sarah Smith, and several hired farmhands.

Luella was a good student. In the "High School Notes" in the December 18, 1897 edition of *Burlington Free Press*, she's listed as a student at the head of her class in Latin and English. As a young adult, she studied nursing at the Mary Fletcher Hospital in Burlington, Vermont. The hospital, which had been founded nearly three decades before with a $200,000 donation from Mary Fletcher, an invalid who suffered from tuberculosis for the majority of her lifetime, had a fine reputation. Fletcher's donation was the largest in Vermont history and established Burlington's first public hospital, the largest hospital that had been built in northern New England at that time.

Luella received her nursing certificate from the hospital program on July 6, 1906.

According the 1910 Census, at the age of twenty-three, Luella was still a member of the Wheeler household and was working as a trained nurse for "private families." Nurses had existed throughout history, but the idea of nursing as a profession was fairly new. By the end of the nineteenth century, nursing programs offered training from six weeks to three years in duration.

At the time, nurses were taught in a variety of places, including hospitals, as you'd suspect, but even local schools, private residences and through correspondence courses. For this reason, nurses' skills were inconsistent, which led to a care environment in which expectations were often unrealistic. Care facilities realized that rules and regular oversight were needed in order to protect both the patients and the nurses who cared for them. The first nurse licensure laws went into effect in the United States in 1903.

In 1911, the *Burlington Free Press* stated that Luella was enduring a long bout of pneumonia. Thankfully, she eventually recovered and gained employment as the night superintendent at Mary Fletcher Hospital. It is unclear how long Luella worked at Mary Fletcher, but, as it went for thousands of other nurses, she followed her patriotism when the United States formally entered World War I in 1917.

There were only 403 nurses in the army nurse corps when the war began, but this was not nearly enough. Over 22,400 professionally trained female nurses were recruited by the American Red Cross to serve in the U.S. Army between 1917 and 1919. More than 10,000 of these nurses served near the western front, and over 1,500 served in the U.S. Navy.

Mary Fletcher Hospital. *Photograph courtesy of Thea Lewis.*

Where did this large number of nurses come from? Their recruitment was the result of a campaign by the army to recruit at least 1,000 nurses per week. Posters that portrayed nurses as sexy, compassionate saviors sprang up and spewed messages like "Are You A Girl With a Star Spangled Heart?" Almost overnight, nursing became an attractive pastime to young women across the United States. The director of the Bureau of Red Cross Nursing, Clara Noyes, complained to a colleague: "Everyone seems to have gone mad. There are moments when I wonder whether we can stem the tide and control the hysterical desire on the part of thousands, literally thousands, to get into nursing....The most vital thing in the life of our profession is the protection of the use of the word nurse..." Still, the need for nurses was great, so standards were developed. A Volunteer Nurses' Aide Service was launched to train young women to assist nurses who were being bombarded with injured soldiers. The criteria for military nurses was strict; applicants to the American Red Cross' armed forces nurse corps had to be between twenty-five and thirty-five years of age, unmarried and graduates of hospital training schools that had more than fifty beds.

In 1917, President Woodrow Wilson appointed Mary Adelaide Nutting, a Canadian citizen, to a chair on the committee on nursing for the medical board of the Council of National Defense. Nutting led the effort in ensuring that there were enough nurses and adequate resources to treat patients during the war effort. When the war ended, Nutting was awarded with the Liberty Science Medal, to commend her for her patriotism and devotion to the war effort. After Luella joined the war effort, she served as a Red Cross nurse and was stationed at Camp MacArthur in Waco, Texas. On September 13, 1918, Louella Wheeler was sent to France with the American Expeditionary Force, which, under General John J. Pershing, launched America's first major offensive in Europe as an independent army. This was a turning point for the allies.

Nursing may have seemed glamorous to the untried, but army nurses knew it was anything but. They suffered homesickness; few had ever left their hometowns, let alone traveled to a foreign country. They made their way across the ocean under constant threat of danger, including blackouts and enemy submarines. While they were encamped, the nurses lived in wooden barracks and slept on hammocks, rather than mattresses. There was dirt, and mud and blood—curlers and permanent waves would have to wait until they made it back to the states. They sometimes shampooed using their helmets as a basin to hold water. Still, while they were subject to inclement weather, close to enemy lines and working in tents and the remnants of bombed-out buildings, they nursed the wounded and the sick. The nurses were paid half the salary of an army private, they held no rank and they were there for the duration of the war. But they made the best of a bad situation—they were saving human lives.

One nurse, Emma Elizabeth Weaver, kept a journal of her experiences; 200 legal-sized documents chronicle her more than two years overseas in 109 cities and towns in Great Britain, Belgium, France, the Netherlands and Germany. After a period on New York's Ellis Island, where she awaited a transport to France, Weaver sailed aboard *Leviathan*. At that time, it was the largest ship afloat and was able to transport 20,000 troops at one time. Of her voyage, she wrote:

> *If the wind came in a certain direction, we could hear the roar of the big guns. We were in constant danger of gas attack and always slept with our gas masks at the head of our bed. Nurses* [at the hospital] *had suffered intense hardships the preceding winter, suffering intensely from the cold. They had chilblains and frozen feet. Many of them were ill with the flu. One of them* [Miss Maria Bowles] *died from scarlet fever.*

Once she was on the ground in Europe, Weaver's days were filled with a constant flow of wounded. They arrived by Red Cross trains, each train carrying around three hundred patients. She wrote:

> *During Miss Williams absence on surgical team, I had charge of Ward A. At this time, the doctors were busy in the operating room practically day and night, consequently, the nurses had to do the dressings on the ward. All day long, from morning until night, I went from bedside to bedside doing dressings. I had an orderly to assist me. He wheeled the dressing carriage, removed bandages, etc. Strenuous days. These patients were rushed directly from the front. I always dreaded removing bandages for fear of hemorrhage. I never knew what I was going to find. There were many missing limbs, horrible deep wounds.*

Leaves were rarely granted, but during one of hers, Elizabeth traveled through Europe, stopping at the battlefields of Soissons, France, where the Allies had suffered 107,000 casualties.

> *It was a harassing sight, ruin and destruction everywhere. It was very dangerous, for so many unexploded shells lay about. (Two sailor boys*

had been killed the previous day by unexploded shells.) Machine guns and machine gun bullets and hand grenades lay everywhere. A pair of boots lay on the ground. I stooped to see to what country they belonged, but I could not turn them over, the feet were still within them and steel helmets lay strewn about. Oh, the horrible war with its carnage and bloodshed.

The history of World War I is full of inspiring stories of nurses who overcame the seemingly insurmountable odds of the conflict. One such story is that of Linnie Leckrone, who was part of a small gas and shock team working in France. She was expected to receive a Citation Star for her efforts, but she was discharged from the army before it was formally presented. Her bravery and composure in caring for the wounded in the face of a devastating artillery attack went unrecognized until her valiant service was commended posthumously, in 2007, with a silver star, the third-highest award for bravery that is granted by the U.S. Armed Forces. Leckrone was one of the first three women who served in World War I to receive it. Her daughter, Mary Jane Bolles Reed, accepted the award in her place.

Another famed World War I nurse was Lenah Higbee. Higbee joined the U.S. Navy Nurse Corps in 1908, when female nurses were not highly regarded and were treated like pariahs among the enlisted. Mostly shunned and with no rank, the talented and compassionate Higbee persevered and was quickly appointed chief nurse. Soon, she was promoted to superintendent of the nurse corps; she was only the second woman to hold the position. She was also the first female to be awarded the Navy Cross for her devotion to the cause and her patients during World War I. She was further honored after her death, when a naval combat ship was christened USS *Higbee*; it was the first U.S. naval vessel to be named after a female service member.

An estimated four hundred nurses from the United States died during World War I—either from disease, accidents or enemy actions. In January 1919, Luella Wheeler was still at Camp Hospital No. 12 in Valdahon, near the German border in western France, but she was there as a patient, not as a nurse. The camp hospital comprised three stone buildings and was supposed to have a maximum capacity of three hundred patients. During the time Luella was there, the hospital was filled not just with wounded, but with soldiers in various stages of Spanish influenza, an unusually infectious strain of the flu that infected five hundred million people around the world. Overcrowded medical camps and hospitals were perfect breeding grounds for the flu. The majority of deaths that occurred during the pandemic, which spanned from 1918 to 1919, were not caused by the virus; most victims died due to the bacterial pneumonia that followed their infections. Luella Wheeler died on January 14, 1919, and though her medical records indicate bronchopneumonia as the cause of her death, it's more likely that she was a victim of the Spanish flu.

Luella's body was transported back to the United States for burial in her family's plot at Lakeview Cemetery. Before her body was interred, Luella's funeral was held at St. Paul's Cathedral in Burlington; it was attended by members of the American Legion and a delegation from the American Legion Ladies Auxiliary. There was also a delegation from the local nurses' home and representatives from the Mary Fletcher Hospital present. At the cemetery, a firing squad from Fort Ethan Allen fired a three-volley salute, a custom originating from Europe. During Europe's dynastic wars, fighting would cease so the dead and wounded could be removed from the battlefields; once the field was clear, three shots were fired into the air to signal that the battle could resume. "Taps" was sounded over her grave. She was survived by her parents and five of her brothers and sisters.

The hospital's Graduate Nurses Association adopted a resolution to extend formal condolences to Luella's family, noting she was a person of ability and integrity, "A woman of...splendid spirit and high ideals; a Christian character." Soon after her death, the Mary Fletcher Alumni Association met to discuss regular business and the creation of a suitable memorial for the well-regarded nurse. (The report in the *Burlington Free Press* notes that, after club business, the guests were treated to "readings by Miss Miriam Bartlett, and selections on a talking machine.") The alumni meeting in which Luella's memorial was planned was held at Burlington's Athena Club. The meeting had the largest number participants in the club's history, with forty-eight places set. Luella's memorial was created in the form of an inscribed clock, which was placed in the hospital in her honor.

20

ADMIRAL HENRY T. MAYO

THE IDEAL SUPERIOR OFFICER

Burlington saw one of the largest military events in its history on May 26, 1937, with the funeral of Admiral Henry Thomas Mayo. His body, which was lying in state in Burlington's City Hall Auditorium and attended at all times by an honor guard, traveled that morning to Lakeview Cemetery. Stores across the city prepared to close, and schools ceased studying the "three R's" (not "reduce, reuse and recycle," but "readin', 'ritin' and 'rithmetic") in order to conduct brief memorials as the long line of troops followed Mayo's flag-draped casket to Lakeview Cemetery on Burlington's North Avenue. Mayo's military escort included the 1st Squadron; 3rd Cavalry; 7th Field Artillery; Headquarters and 2nd Battalion; the 13th Infantry from Fort Devens, Massachusetts; and one Battalion of the 172nd Infantry of the Vermont National Guard. An attachment of Burlington Police Department, along with clergymen, actual pallbearers and fifteen honorary pallbearers (that included prominent businessmen, admirals—both active and retired— brigadier generals, former mayors and at least one supreme court justice) also accompanied the casket. The 7th Field Artillery Band played, as did the 13th Infantry Band from Fort Devens. At the grave, "Taps" was played by a bugler from the Portsmouth Navy Yard. As a special consideration for the admiral's funeral procession, Burlington's chief of police, Victor Fisher, requested that the streets along the route be cleared of parked cars between the hours of 6:00 a.m. and 11:00 a.m. that day.

As you may have guessed, the admiral was kind of a big deal. Mayo was born on December 8, 1856, to a family that was no stranger to the water or the military. His father, who was also named Henry, was born in Orwell, Vermont, on December 13, 1802. At the age of ten, during the War of 1812, Henry relocated, with his parents, to Burlington, which remained his home base for the rest of his eighty-seven years. In the early 1800s, the Mayo family business was baking. The admiral's grandfather and uncle owned a store on Maple Street in Burlington that was contracted to provide bread for the U.S. Army, which camped close by, at what is now Burlington's Battery Park. As he grew, Henry, the elder, began building a reputation as a sailor on a ship called *Phoenix*, a sidewheel paddle steamer that ran on Lake Champlain, between New York, Vermont, and present-day Quebec.

Henry Sr. eventually left the lake to become a junior partner in a mercantile business called Davis and Mayo on Burlington's Water Street (Battery Street today). He was engaged in merchandising for a few years before he eventually went off on his own, but the lake was calling, and he returned to steam boating in 1847. He was a popular lake captain and, at different times, was in command of the steamers *Boston*, *Montreal* and *Saranac*, as well as the ships *America* and *A. Williams*.

He and his wife, Elizabeth (Eldridge), had nine children, with Henry, the second youngest, coming in at the back of the pack. In his boyhood, people said Henry Mayo was slender, with a mop of blonde curls and that he liked to hang around the lake shore. He was mischievous and loved pulling pranks. He also loved to read and could often be found sitting on a hassock with a book, totally oblivious to the world around him. At the tender age of sixteen, he was nominated to a vacancy at the U.S. Naval Academy in Annapolis by Congressman Smith, who noted he had aced his examinations and would make a "bold sailor boy." He graduated from the academy in 1876.

In 1881, as Ensign Mayo, he married Miss Mary Caroline "Carrie" Wing, who was a daughter of Burlington Lieutenant H.R. Wing, a Burlington alderman. The *Burlington Free Press* wrote:

> *The church was filled to its utmost last evening on the pleasant occasion of the marriage of Miss Carrie Wing, daughter of ex-alderman H.R. Wing, and Ensign Henry T. Mayo, U.S.N., son of Captain Henry Mayo of this city. The platform and pulpit were handsomely decorated with flowers in pots and floral emblems, the desk being surmounted by a large horseshoe of exotics. The Reverend Safford performed the ceremony, assisted by Reverend W.B. Wilcox.*

Admiral Henry T.
Mayo. *Photograph courtesy
of the Library of Congress.*

The couple had two sons: Chester, and George, who both, in adulthood, served in the armed forces.

In 1883, as an ensign on the ship *Yantic*, Mayo was part of the relief effort for the Greeley Expedition, also known as the Lady Franklin Bay Expedition. The United States was keen to beat the "farthest north" record that had been achieved by the British, and they put Greeley, a man with scant knowledge of the Arctic or its weather conditions, in charge of twenty-five men tasked with collecting scientific data in there. The poorly planned trip was an example of the old expression "Whatever can go wrong will go wrong." The expedition resulted in twenty-four deaths, cannibalism and a halt in collaborations between explorers of that region for generations. From 1895 to 1898, Mayo helped survey Pearl Harbor in the hydrographic vessel *Bennington*.

On April 9, 1914, Mexican authorities seized an unarmed party of U.S. sailors while they were ashore at the port of Tampico. Mayo upped his credibility and profile, which were already high, when he demanded a formal, public apology from the Mexican authorities for their actions.

When the Mexican authorities refused, President Woodrow Wilson issued instructions to seize the Mexican customs house at Vera Cruz. It was the beginning of the end for Mexican dictator General Victoriano Huerta, who wasn't able to throw his weight around for much longer.

In 1915, Mayo was promoted to vice admiral. Throughout World War I, Admiral Mayo commanded the Atlantic fleet, and in August 1917, he traveled to London to discuss Allied naval co-operation and the construction of the Northern Barrage and anti-U-boat minefield. There was plenty of official business to occupy him, but, as he always did while he was away, he wrote letters to his wife, Carrie, including the one below, which contains reminders that he will "enlarge the conversation" with her about his trip once he arrived back in the United States.

Admiral Henry T. Mayo, Commander-In-Chief, Atlantic Fleet,
To Caroline Wing Mayo

Carlton Hotel
London, Sept. 27, 1917

My own dear Carrie:

You have been neglected, but it was unavoidable. As it is now certain that my letter will go on the steamer that takes us, I will simply jot down the main points of the happenings of each day so that they may be reminders on which to enlarge in conversation. We left Calais at 8:40 a.m. Tuesday, arriving at Dunkirk about 10:00. We were met by Admiral Ronnark, French Navy, the French general commanding and some British naval officers representing Vice Admiral Bacon and were taken in autos to the harbor pier. The British Flotilla leader "Broke" arrived a few minutes later from Dover, bringing Admiral Jellicoe and Vice Admiral Bacon. The latter commands all the British naval forces in Dover and along the north French coast and Flanders. After they arrived, we were taken to see some British naval batteries on shore, then to a hotel for lunch. After lunch, we went out to the big British aviation station—where they have about 400 machines. Dunkirk was heavily bombed in the air raid of the previous night, and the Huns did tremendous damage at this station. It is said that the population of Dunkirk is being rapidly reduced. People do not like the air raids and are getting out. We saw much evidence of damage done—buildings shattered, windows gone, etc. From the aviation station, we went back and on board H.M.S. Broke saw a new style of C.M. boat of great speed and carrying a single torpedo inspected a mine net laid out for the purpose. Then we went to sea and toward Ostend. There, a monitor was in position, a smoke screen was being laid as we approached. Destroyer patrols were out, aeroplane spotters were in the air and aeroplane fighters also, and the monitor began a bombardment of Ostend. Soon, the Germans woke up and began to reply, and there were shells dropping in our direction, some of which fell quite near us. We spent an hour or so—probably less—there then steamed off, toward Dover. Stopped to look at the net barrage near the Goodwin Sands, then into Dover harbor. Found a special drawn up on the track abreast where we landed—and we were soon off for London. Just then, the approach of five enemy aeroplanes toward Dover was reported. The train was held up a bit by a freight car off the track and then went very slowly so as not to reach London during the air raid. We had dinner in the car, about 9:30, the air raid was reported over, so we went more rapidly and reached London at 10:30 p.m. I came right to the hotel and turned in. Yesterday was a full da…I went to the embassy at 10:00 a.m. and waited some time for Ambassador Page then had quite a lark with him. From the embassy, I went to Sims's office and was there until I had to leave to keep an appointment with Admiral Jellicoe at the admiralty. He gave me a lot of papers, which he wanted me to read over before leaving. Had lunch at the hotel at 1:30, then wrote notes of thanks to various officials in France who had been nice to us during our visit—then read a portion of Jellicoe's papers. Arrangements had been made for the king to receive me at 6:00 p.m., and at 5:45, Admiral Everett, who is a king's aid, came for me and we went to the palace (Buckingham). There, a gentleman in waiting received us and were seated in the "Oriental room" until the king was ready for me. We were a little early, as is usual. At 6:00 promptly, I was informed that the King was ready to receive me. I was escorted to the door by Sir—something or other—and introduced and then left with the king, who gave me a chair, sat down with me, and we had a chat for about fifteen minutes. I liked him—and there was no fuss or anything of the kind. He had a good deal to say about the German air raid of Monday night—when one bomb dropped near the palace—one very close to the Parliament Building and a number in east London. Then the war was discussed, the attitude and assistance of the U.S., etc.—and the interview was over. I came back to the hotel, read the evening papers and went to Mall House for an 8:00 dinner with Admiral Jellicoe. The

*other guests were Lord Balfour, Rear Admiral Duff and Commander
King. Had a most pleasant time—Lady Jellicoe, who had been out in the
country, came about 9:00 p.m. We left her at the table and went to the
drawing room, and she only came in there for a minute later on. I got back
to the Hotel at 10:30, turned in and read papers until nearly midnight.
This morning, I have been writing more notes, have had a conference with
Sims, have filed up some cable messages to send, etc. At 3:00 p.m., I have
a final conference with Admiral Jellicoe. Must make a farewell call on
the first lord, have tea with Lady Browning, call on Ambassador and
Mrs. Page—leave cards on various naval officers, have dinner at 7:00
and leave for Queenstown between 8:00 and 9:00. The* St. Louis *sails
on Monday, October 1—from Liverpool.*

*I love you, my own Carrie!
Yours ever,
Henry*

Mayo's leadership during World War I earned him the Navy Distinguished
Service Medal. After the war, he urged an increase in military air power with
the further development of naval aviation. Following the war, Mayo served
as chairman of the U.S. Navy's General Board—where he was a proponent
of smaller warship construction. He retired from the navy in 1921, retaining
his commission as an admiral by a 1930 act of Congress. Admiral Mayo
died at Portsmouth, New Hampshire, on February 23, 1937, at the home of
his son, Captain Chester G. Mayo. He was eighty years old.

21

JUDGE EDMUND CURTIS MOWER

A MIGHTY RESUME

Whether he was great or not, Judge E.C. Mower did have an impressive resume. In his lifetime, he was a lawyer, a state's attorney and a municipal judge. He was also night editor of the *Burlington Free Press*, a banker, a lecturer and a professor emeritus of political science at the University of Vermont. He later became a senator, served on the state board of bar examiners and was the head of the board of Burlington's Fletcher Free Library. Beyond that, Mower was an active Unitarian, a Freemason, a Rotarian and a member of Burlington's Ethan Allen Club, an all-male social organization that sprang from the volunteer fire team, the Ethan Allen Engine Company. Before he turned to teaching at the University of Vermont, the Morrisville, Vermont native was an author of a book on constitutional law. Mower was also a temporary faculty member at Northwestern University and the University of California, Los Angeles.

In the courtroom, Mower was tough. When he was preparing to decide what to do about Katie Hathaway, a Burlington woman described by the *Burlington Free Press* as a "star drunkard" and who had been in his court so many times that "the novelty had worn off," the judge asked, "…why don't you leave drink alone? The officers would not be after you if you would stop drinking." When the woman avoided his gaze and fidgeted with her gloves, he continued, "You are a habitual drunkard, and there is nothing left for me but to give you the maximum punishment prescribed by law. The sentence of the court is that you be fined $15.00 and costs of $9.93 and that you also be confined in jail for a period of thirty days." He also gave a woman, who was identified only as "Mrs. Martin" no less than four and no more than five months in jail after she pled guilty on charges of running a "house of ill fame." Incorrigible boys who found themselves in front of Mower's bench for skipping school or stealing were often sent to the Vermont Reform School in Vergennes.

Still, Mower was a staunch advocate for judicial reform and the right to a speedy trial, not just for the victims' sake but to promote efficiency of the courts. Britain's expeditious handling of criminal offenses was a favorite example of his. He also worked to change the court system to make allowances for the age of the defendant, since, before the advent of the juvenile court, children as young as seven were considered nothing more than tiny adults and could be tried as such. In 1925, during a Prohibition-era crime wave, he gave a speech at the University of Chicago, which his obituary in the *New York Times* quoted.

> *Unhappily, it is getting to be a trite saying that among all the so-called civilized peoples of the modern world, we Americans are the most lawless. The charge is pressed against us not only as an indication of the breakdown of our criminal justice, but also by the more pessimistic to bolster up the contention that democracy, because it will not respect its laws, is doomed to failure.*

Despite his many pursuits, Judge Mower did find time to marry. He tied the knot with Maud E. Dodds, and the couple had three children: Marshall, Edmund and Margaret. The judge died on April 25, 1940, at the age of seventy-one, after an illness that lasted for several weeks. His funeral was held at his home at 204 South Willard Street.

22

JOHN J. FLYNN

THE NEGOTIATOR

If any man won the right to be called the financial wizard of Vermont,
that man was John J. Flynn.
—Burlington Free Press, *September 13, 1940*

John J. Flynn was born on June 22, 1854, in Dorset, Vermont, the son of James Flynn and his wife, Catherine (Shea) Flynn, who immigrated from Ireland as a young married couple. John dropped out of school at a tender age, and when he was barely in his teens, he traveled to Burlington, hoping to find work. He was soon employed by James A. Shedd, who owned a dairy farm, and he began delivering milk around town. The whip-smart youngster kept his eyes and ears open, learning all he could about the business. A year later, while still in his mid-teens, John was managing the farm. A year after that, he leased the place.

In 1877, John married Nellie F. Waite of Dorset, a botanist who was a colleague of C.G. Pringle of Charlotte, Vermont. (Pringle has been listed as one of the top five historical botanists in the United States for the quantity of species he discovered.) Nellie mainly collected samples in the vicinity of Burlington and Nantucket, Massachusetts. She predeceased Flynn on December 9, 1922. Her book *The Flora of Burlington and Vicinity* (1935) was published posthumously by Flynn.

While he was still in his twenties, Flynn decided to expand into the retail grocery business, joining up with W.B. McKillip, who remained Flynn's lifelong business associate. Six years later, Flynn bought twenty-seven thousand acres of land and built a turnpike from Peru, Vermont, to Manchester. It operated as a toll road, and he later sold it to the state. Flynn was keen on the modernization of public amenities, from energy to transportation. The development of these conveniences fascinated and engaged him for half a century. Flynn built the Burlington Traction Company, which served much of the county with rail service, and organized the Military Post Street Railway. He also organized and financed the Barre and Montpelier Street Railway System, the Clyde River Power Company, the St. Albans and Swanton Electric Lines, the Barre Gas Plant, the hydroelectric station of the Vergennes Electric Company and more. He was also the president, director and officer of so many companies that it could make anyone's head spin: the Chittenden Trust Company, which he founded in 1901; the Vermont Milk Chocolate Company; the Elias Lyman Coal Company; the Burlington Building and Loan Company; the Burlington Federal Savings and Loan; the Mutual Fire Insurance Company; Queen City Realty; and the Capital, Majestic and Flynn Theaters.

As a member of numerous commissions and as a booster of as many charitable institutions, Flynn never forgot his humble beginnings, and he had a particular soft spot for the underprivileged youth of the city. The annual New Year dinners that he hosted for the area's newsboys, messengers and errand boys were legendary. Hundreds of kids gathered at posh dining

A messenger boy with L.W. Hines. *Photograph courtesy of the Library of Congress.*

The Flynn Theater, circa 1932.
Photograph courtesy of the University of Vermont, Special Collections.

rooms in local hotels for turkey dinners with all of the fixings, including dessert and tickets to a local theater Flynn owned. One year, the number of guests topped one thousand, and the party had to be held in two hotels.

In January 1928, the community- and profit-minded Flynn banded together with two other Burlington businessmen to persuade the Robinson Brothers, whose home base was Canada, not to move their broom handle company to the town of Swanton. Swanton was offering a sweet deal for the company's relocation: Free power for three years, half-price power for the next five and no local taxes for ten years. Flynn, Roy L. Patrick and Thomas Unsworth, who were all friends of the brothers, pointed out the pitfalls of moving to Swanton, including that Burlington had better shipping facilities. The three capped a deal for a factory with a new, more attractive ten-year lease. One hundred jobs were saved.

In 1929, a fire on Main Street destroyed one of J.J. Flynn's real estate properties. Flynn, who was traveling at the time, told the local paper he wasn't too concerned; the building was insured, and he'd been planning to gut it, anyway, to build a theater. The Flynn Theater, which is now a jewel in Burlington's crown, was a point of contention among the city's other businessmen. The problem was that Flynn's plans for his new block put the building fifty-four inches over the city line, twice the allowance of nearby buildings. Flynn made ample use of his position in the city and his Irish charm when he argued that he was only using the original foundation—that of the LaFrance Hotel—which had been there for over one hundred years. Others in the vicinity had used their existing foundations, and he couldn't help it if his didn't meet the new city code. The city building inspector, when Flynn asked him about the design, had told him to go ahead; now, he was in danger of having to start all over again.

Flynn was generous with his time, money and even his land. He owned an estate near Starr Farm Road in Burlington's New North End, and he leased out parcels for thirty-two summer cottages. Stories say that John J. Flynn could be opinionated. He liked what he liked and hated what he didn't. But if he took a shine to you and believed in you—or in the good you could do—he was your staunchest advocate. He was a member of the Algonquin Club, the Ethan Allen Club and Burlington Lodge No. 916 of the Benevolent Protective Order of Elks, and he served on a variety of local commissions.

John J. Flynn died on September 12, 1940, at the Mary Fletcher Hospital, just one month after he suffered a cerebral hemorrhage at his home at 251 South Willard Street. He and Nellie had no children. Under the conditions of his will, his estate went to the Medical Center Hospital of Vermont, the Fanny Allen Hospital and Catholic charities.

23

HORATIO NELSON JACKSON

YOU WANNA BET?

N ever underestimate the public relations power of a dog—especially one that wears goggles. This is just one takeaway from the story of Horatio Nelson Jackson, the first man to travel across the span of the continental United States by automobile.

Jackson was born to American parents in Toronto, Ontario, Canada on March 25, 1872. He was the son of Reverend Samuel N. Jackson, a Congregational minister, and Mary Ann (Parklyn) Jackson. As an 1893 graduate of the University of Vermont, he took up medicine and interned at the Mary Fletcher Hospital. He later practiced in the southern Vermont town of Brattleboro at the Brattleboro Retreat, then returned to Burlington and continued to practice medicine there.

When it came time to marry, Jackson chose a society girl named Bertha "Swipes" Richardson Wells, whose father and grandfather were two of the richest men in Vermont, partially due to an elixir called Paine's Celery Tonic. The tonic was manufactured by their pharmaceutical firm, which was touted as the cure-all of its time. The couple's evening wedding ceremony on July 6, 1899, at Burlington's St. Paul's Cathedral was the talk of the town. The bride wore a princess gown of ivory satin "lavishly" trimmed with point à l'aiguille lace, the most filmy and delicate of all point lace. On her head, she wore a tulle veil attached to a coronet of *real* orange blossoms. Her bridesmaids' gowns were pink with blonde lace, and they wore feathered headdresses to match. They carried bouquets of lily of the valley, tied together with pink chiffon ribbons. A tasteful reception was held at the Wells Mansion

Dr. Horatio N. Jackson. *Photograph courtesy of the Library of Congress.*

on Willard Street, and no expense was spared. Delmonico's of New York catered the event.

By all indications, Jackson adored Bertha, who was nicknamed "Swipes," and she was crazy about him. At any rate, she must have been an understanding and adventurous spouse. After their wedding, Jackson gave up practicing medicine, and he and Bertha went on an extended tour of Europe. They continued to enjoy traveling throughout their union. In May 1903, the pair was just capping a winter in California with a visit to San Francisco when Jackson, who was a guest at an exclusive, all-male university club, began talking with a group of gents about the automobile, and its limitations and benefits. Legend has it that one thing led to another, and a man remarked that it would be impossible to drive a "contraption" like the early auto across the country. Jackson, who didn't even drive, bet him fifty dollars that he could *and* that he could make the whole trip in less than three months. Today, the endeavor might seem like a piece of cake, but in the automobile's infancy, it was a breathtaking concept.

At first, Jackson and Bertha planned to make the trip together and received a crash course in driving from a local chauffeur named Sewell K. Crocker. They ended up deciding that Bertha would travel back to New England by rail, while Jackson made the trip with Crocker. That way, Jackson's beloved Swipes would be home to help coordinate the East coast leg of his trip. Jackson begrudgingly said goodbye to her at the station; a three-months absence from one another would be hard for both of them, but he was determined, and she agreed. She traveled back home with the two cars that they'd bought for tooling around the Queen City, and he prepared for his trip.

Jackson was thirty-one years old, and Crocker was just twenty-two when they started off on their journey on May 23, 1903, on a northern route, from San Francisco to New York, in the Winton automobile that Jackson dubbed the *Vermont*. The very first car sold in America had hit the road only seven years before Jackson's trip, and it was generally thought that the roads in the United States were "inferior to those of any civilized country," according to at least one journalist. Of the 2.3 million miles of roads in the United States at that time, only about 150 of them were paved. Ford's 1908 mass production of the Model T created a desire for better roads in the United States. While some of the roads that Jackson and Crocker traveled may have had a thin layer of gravel on top, most were dirt roads—rutted and muddy.

It was a bumpy ride for the two men and their equipment, which included spare tires and inner tubes, gas cans, all-weather camping gear (including

Horatio N. Jackson with Sewall K. Crocker and Bud, the dog. *Photograph courtesy of the Library of Congress.*

sleeping bags), two suitcases, a medicine cabinet, some books, some fishing gear, guns, a Kodak box camera and a telescope. They were only a few miles outside of town when they changed their first tire. The gas they used was the same that was used for heating stoves, and it was readily available at hardware stores along the way. The Winton wasn't exactly energy efficient at seven miles to the gallon. The pair drove along the Oregon Trail, which was, at that time, still rutted by the wheels of Conestoga wagons. They crossed mountain passes with little clearance, and they sometimes had to stop to move boulders out of the way. They encountered plenty of curious folks, like the ones mentioned in Horatio's letter to Bertha, which was written on May 25, 1903.

We met a red-haired young woman riding along on a white horse.

"Which way to Marysville?" I asked her.

"Right down that road," she said and pointed. We took that road for… miles, and then it came to a dead end at an isolated farmhouse. The family all turned out to stare at us and told us we'd have to go back.

We went back and met the red-haired young woman again.

"Why did you send us way down there?" I asked her.

"I wanted paw and maw and my husband to see you," she said. "They've never seen an automobile."

In Idaho, the pair met Bud, a photogenic pit bull who took his place on the seat between Nelson and Crocker, his goggles wrapped behind his ears. His face was soon splashed across the front pages of newspapers across the country, and readers loved the canine star, who further humanized the daring duo.

Jackson wrote Bertha regularly. His letter to her on July 5, the day before their anniversary, was especially sweet.

My darling Swipes,

We expected our express on No. 5 at three this afternoon, but a message this noon from the train agent says that he has nothing, so it is another day. It has been an awful long time to us, and I shall be mighty glad when we are on the way again…and unless another serious accident happens, we ought to be able to make good time across these plains…

Well, tomorrow is our anniversary, and I wish I could be with you. I want to celebrate here by getting my new parts. I shall think of you a good deal tomorrow, as I always do. You are the best little wife in the world, and I am a mighty lucky fellow to have you.

Yes, old girl, I appreciate it, if, sometimes I have a queer way of showing it.

Four years tomorrow!!!! They have been very short and dear ones to me. You have done everything in the world to make me happy.

I shall just tear up the ground until I can be with you. With lots of love to all I am yours.

Nelson

Once the pair reached New York, they were determined not to stop for anything. News of their arrival brought out crowds of cheering locals, who had followed their progress in the local papers. After a last interruption to their journey—a blown tire— Nelson and Crocker reached Bertha, officials from the Winton Engine Company and a crowd of reporters in Peekskill, New York. With an entourage, they reached Manhattan at 4:30 a.m. on July 26. It was sixty-three days, twelve hours and thirty minutes after their cross-country escapade began. The July 27 *New York Herald* documented their arrival.

> *Dr. H. Nelson Jackson and Sewall K. Crocker, his chauffeur, finished the first transcontinental automobile trip at half-past four o'clock yesterday morning.*
>
> *On their arrival, the mud-besmirched and travel-stained vehicle, which had borne them so faithfully and sturdily over fifty-six hundred miles of roads between the Pacific and the Atlantic, was housed in a garage in West 58th Street. All day yesterday, it was visited by admiring automobilists, and curious passersby peeped in upon it. In honor of its achievement, it was decorated with tiny flags and draped with national standards.*
>
> *The thick coating of mud gave evidence that it had been somewhere and that, somewhere a long way off, a broken mud guard and a sprung front axle alone attested the hard knocks it had had on its long journey.*

Nelson and Crocker celebrated for several days until Jackson grew tired of it all, got in his car and headed north to the Green Mountains. He'd spent about $8,000 to win a $50 bet. It's unclear whether that amount includes the ticket he got when he reached Burlington for traveling through the city going faster than the six-mile-per-hour speed limit. He was the first person ever to be ticketed for such an offense—another record. When he was asked some years later if he remembered the incident, he said he did. The ticket had cost him $13, and ever since, thirteen was his lucky number.

Jackson continued to live a more than comfortable life in Burlington, Vermont, with Bertha and his pal Bud, who became a familiar sight on the streets of Burlington. He gave up doctoring for business and worked as the managing director of mining properties in Mexico, Arizona and Alaska. He was also involved in the Barre, Vermont granite company that was owned by his brother, Hollister.

When World War I broke out, Jackson, a long-time member of the National Guard, was considered, at the age of forty-six, too old for active service. He disagreed. With the influence of former president Theodore Roosevelt, whom he'd met through a mutual friend, Jackson was placed on active duty as a captain in the medical corps, and he eventually attained the rank of major. He proved to be an invaluable addition to the war effort, caring for the wounded and administering first aid, even in the face of heavy shell fire. He carried on with his duties through ever-present danger until he was wounded himself. His awards included the Distinguished Service Cross for "extraordinary heroism," the Purple Heart and France's Croix de Guerre, or "Cross of War."

After the war, Jackson became a colonel in the officer reserve corps and was one of the founders of the American Legion, a patriotic veterans organization chartered by Congress in 1919. Jackson never held public office, but he did once run for governor of Vermont in a three-way race, coming in second to popular lieutenant governor George D. Aiken.

In 1921, Jackson, who was always forward-thinking and interested in media, bought a newspaper, the *Burlington Daily News*, and a radio station with the call letters WCAX (now WVMT), which he later sold to Charles Phillips Hasbrook. Hasbrook, with his stepson, Stuart T. Martin, eventually took the WCAX call letters for Vermont's first television station, the CBS affiliate WCAX-TV. In his later years, Jackson served as the president of the Burlington Trust Company.

Horatio N. Jackson with his wife, Bertha, and brother, Hollister. *Photograph courtesy of the Library of Congress.*

Tragedy struck when Jackson's brother S. Hollister Jackson who was then the lieutenant governor of Vermont, lost his life in Vermont's Great Flood of 1927. At the time, the lieutenant governor was headed to his home in Barre, Vermont, when his car hit a deep hole and stalled as he attempted to make his way through the fast-rising waters of the Potash Brook. Witnesses said that, as he began walking toward his house, a rush of deep and swiftly moving water carried him away. It seems that most of the Jackson brothers were politically minded. Another brother, Dr. J. Holmes Jackson, a Burlington dentist, was mayor of Burlington, Vermont, from 1917 to 1925, and again from 1929 to 1933.

Jackson and Bertha had one daughter, who they named after Bertha's mother. The girl was the biological child of Jackson's brother Dr. Joseph Addison Jackson and Eva (Fairbank) Jackson, who, at the time of the child's birth, were already parents to Mary A. Parkyn Jackson. It's unclear why Bertha, and not Mary, was adopted by her aunt and uncle at an early age. Bertha Richardson Wells Jackson, the younger, eventually became an editor for the *Burlington Daily News*; she was one of the first woman editors in the country. For a time, she was the only female member of the Associated Press

Horatio N. Jackson's monument at Lakeview Cemetery. *Photograph courtesy of Thea Lewis.*

of New England. She married George B. Kolk, who worked for the Veteran's Administration, and they had three children.

On his eightieth birthday, Jackson was celebrated in the ballroom of Burlington's Hotel Vermont for his contributions to the American Legion. According to an article in the *Burlington Free Press*, the Legion, which was in the middle of a statewide membership drive, hoped to present to Jackson at the event "the largest enrollment of members in the state's history."

The elder Bertha Jackson died at her home at 128 South Willard Street in Burlington at the age of eighty-one. Her death occurred on December 14, 1954, the birthday of her beloved father, Brigadier General William Wells, and it came after a long illness. Her obituary remembered her as member of many clubs and societies, including the Veterans of Foreign Wars Ladies Auxiliary. Her funeral was held at her home, and she was buried in her family's plot at Lakeview Cemetery. And, as though he couldn't bear to be without her any longer, Horatio Nelson Jackson died one month, to the day, after the passing of his wife, on January 14, 1955, at Burlington's DeGosbriand Hospital at the age of eighty-two. The *Burlington Free Press* noted in one tribute that his life was "one of action." Perhaps his record-breaking road trip, which he successfully completed despite daily adversities and every imaginable breakdown and delay, taught him to just keep going.

24

STILLMAN MORGAN ATHERTON GILLETTE

TWA FLIGHT 3

1940s Hollywood was the land of dreams, even if acting wasn't your goal. For one young Burlington man, who is now buried in Lakeview Cemetery, his dream ended in a nightmare, a fiery plane crash in the dark Nevada Mountains. It was an accident that also ended the life of a beloved star of the silver screen.

Stillman-Morgan Atherton Gillette was born on July 24, 1916, to Edgar and Nina May (Atherton) Gillette. He was one of the twenty-two people who perished on Trans World Airlines (TWA) Flight 3 on January 16, 1942, in Clark County, Nevada. Gillette had been employed by Trans World Airlines for a little over a year; he was a co-pilot working on the run between Albuquerque, New Mexico, and Los Angeles, California, on the company's huge Skyliner aircraft. From the time he was a small boy, Gillette was interested in aviation, but it seems that he was a child of many talents. He played trumpet in the school orchestra, and, with his small, two-person sailboat, he took part in snipe races on Malletts Bay in Colchester, Vermont. He also played on the Burlington High School baseball team.

Gillette graduated second in his class from Burlington High School, and he left the city to complete a year at the Riverside military academy in Gainesville, Georgia, and Hollywood, Florida. He attended college at Norwich University in Northfield, Vermont. A December 1937 notice in the *Burlington Free Press* announced his return to his home at Hungerford Terrace in Burlington for the Christmas holiday. He underwent commercial pilot training at the Burlington airport under the instructor and airport manager

Harold Pugh. Pugh was the husband of Grace Hall Pugh, a schoolteacher who became the first licensed female aviator in the state of Vermont. Grace obtained her student flight permit in 1932, a time when, as she put it, "Pilots flew by common sense, and by the seats of their pants," with few instruments, no radio and no tail wheel or brakes.

Gillette obtained his private pilot's license in Vermont but had something bigger in mind. His next step was to complete the flying hours he needed for pilot certification with Trans World Airlines. Gillette graduated second in his class after his TWA training. He became one of the airline's youngest pilots, and he gained a reputation as one of the few pilots based in Burbank, California, who was qualified to fly all of the company's planes. At the time of his ill-fated flight, Gillette was engaged to Joan Allen, a Hollywood girl and the daughter of an engineer whose company manufactured the planes Gillette flew. Their wedding date was January 24, only a week after the crash.

Also on the flight, though she wasn't supposed to be, was movie star Carole Lombard. Lombard, who was originally from Fort Wayne, Indiana, had traveled to her home state by train with her mother, Elizabeth (Bess) Peters, and her agent, Otto Winkler, on a patriot's mission, a war bond drive at Cadle Tabernacle in Indianapolis. Rumor has it that, after raising more than $2 million in defense bonds a single night, Lombard was keen on getting back to Hollywood as quickly as possible. She was soon scheduled to appear at the preview of her new film with Jack Benny, *To Be or Not To Be*, and would soon be starting the production on her next film, *He Kissed the Bride*. Work obligations aside, her husband, Clark Gable, was in the midst of shooting *Somewhere I'll Find You*, with the lovely and much younger Lana Turner, and the Tinsel Town gossip mill was whispering that there was more than acting going on between the two. Lombard wanted to ditch her plans to return to Los Angeles by train. She even told *LIFE Magazine* photographer Myron Davis that she simply couldn't endure "three days on the 'choo choo' train," but there was an obstacle: her mother and her agent were afraid to fly. Lombard suggested they could flip a coin over it—they did, and she won.

At 4:00 a.m., on January 16, the three boarded the cabin of TWA Flight 3 at the Indianapolis Municipal Airport. Most of the other passengers on the twenty-one-seat Douglas Transport headed to Los Angeles were military personnel; and at a scheduled stop in Albuquerque, New Mexico, where the original flight crew was supposed to be switched out, additional servicemen bound for Los Angeles were waiting to board the plane. It was just five weeks after the attack on Pearl Harbor, and wartime rules dictated that the army

Carole Lombard with Clark Gable and her mother, Elizabeth Peters. *Photograph courtesy of the Indy Star.*

air corps flyers on the way to their assignments were essential to the war effort and had priority, even on civilian transportation. Lombard and her party were asked to relinquish their seats, but she wasn't having it. She made a scene, citing the $2 million in bonds she'd just sold in Indiana and the people in high places who had pulled strings to get her on the plane in the first place. The money she raised, she claimed, made *her* essential as well. Four other passengers, who did not yet know that she'd done them a favor, were bumped instead.

When the plane left Albuquerque, it was lower on fuel than it should have been, due to the weight of the equipment carried by the servicemen and the luggage stowed for Lombard and her entourage. A refueling stop had been planned for Winslow, Arizona, because of the load and expected headwinds, but the pilot in command, Captain Wayne C. Williams, an eleven-year employee of TWA, decided to skip it. Instead, the DC-3 made an unscheduled stop for fuel in Las Vegas, at what is now Nellis Air Force Base. The plane took off for Los Angeles around 7:00 p.m., but once it was in the air, the pilot and crew were unable to properly navigate over the mountains surrounding Las Vegas. Their flight plan was skewed due to an error made in the compass, and because of the threat of Japanese aircraft in American airspace, the safety beacons that were once used to direct night flights were turned off. The crew in the cockpit were unable to see the mountains in their flight path. At 7:20 p.m. Pacific Standard Time, Flight DC-3 crashed into "Double Up Peak" on Petosi Mountain. There were no survivors. It is believed that everyone, the passengers and crew members, died instantly.

The wreckage was spread over a wide area, with bits of plane and personal belongings scattered over the snow and clinging to pine trees. It took days to complete the difficult task of removing the bodies from the rocky trail. Today, the crash site draws curious hikers and treasure hunters; people dig holes and leave litter. Stillman-Morgan Gillette and the other twenty-one individuals who lost their lives on the mountain deserve better.

25

B.H. "TOMMY" THOMPSON

GARDENS FOR ALL

B ryson H. "Tommy" Thompson was born in Shelburne, Vermont, on August 11, 1917. He was the son of Thomas M. and Alice (Bryson) Thompson. As a graduate of the Bay Path Business Institute in Springfield, Massachusetts, he went on to work as a terminal manager at a one of Vermont's leading trucking companies, Gay's Express Inc., in Bellows Falls. In 1942, Thompson joined the United States Air Force, and during World War II, he worked as a cryptographic technician, analyzing encrypted electronic communications, deciphering information in foreign languages and maintaining the networks used to generate top-secret intel. In 1942, on August 1, he married Mary Siliski, a bookkeeper from Springfield, Vermont. The couple had a daughter named Marilyn.

When Thompson's tour of duty was over, he entered the restaurant field and opened the popular Top Hat restaurant in Ascutney, Vermont. He operated the restaurant for twenty years before he retired. But it seems that feeding people was destined to be a theme for Tommy. The retired restaurateur joined forces with a company called Garden Way and became the founding director of Gardens for All, a project that was half a job and half a dream. The dream started in 1972 with a man named Lyman Wood, one of the founders of Garden Way, a company known for a product called the Troy-Bilt rear-end tiller, which was manufactured in Troy, New York. Wood's company had a thriving mail-order business, its own publishing company (offering books for country living) and Garden Way Research, which manufactured the nearly ubiquitous Garden Way garden cart, a handy tool that let you load and pull your plants and supplies and gave you a place to sit while you gardened, in Charlotte, Vermont.

Wood, who had started his first company at the age of thirteen, was interested in more than profits. His company name came from his goal to "live the garden way of life." In 1944, he wrote, the "'Have More' Plan," a pamphlet that encouraged people to live off the land. Through his company, Wood funded space for more than 20 garden sites throughout Burlington, and he hired Thompson to coordinate the new community gardening programs. Thompson began looking for vacant lots or private land that could be donated for gardening use. He found them in parcels owned by the city of Burlington, local churches, the University of Vermont and local businesses. He accumulated 21 gardening sites in a few years' time, and people soon began gardening in them. Thompson even managed to finagle the donation of seeds. The plots were able to serve more than 700 families and individuals in the Burlington area. The cost to rent a plot was only ten dollars, or whatever a person could pay. By the end of 1972, the number of community garden plots rose to 540. To Thompson, community gardens only made sense. He once said, "Why buy summer lettuce that has to be shipped from California 3,000 miles away?"

Entrance to the Tommy Thompson gardens. *Photograph courtesy of Thea Lewis.*

In 1975, gardeners learned that they could make the most of their seasonal bounty with advice on preserving from the UVM extension service and a harvest center for canning vegetables, which was located at Shelburne Farms on the historic Webb Estate in Shelburne, Vermont. An article by columnist Maggie Maurice in the *Burlington Free Press* called canning a "sociable way" to "put things by." Instead of canning alone in their own hot kitchens, Burlington residents could go to the center, where everything was provided: sugar, spices, vinegar and wide mouth funnels. The center even provided the equipment gardeners needed for chopping, dicing and pea shelling. There were machines at the center that could peel a peck of potatoes and beets in five minutes—something that was pretty attractive to home chefs who were toiling for hours in summer heat. The center also provided company and recipes. The price to can two quarts or three pints of winter stores was just twenty-five cents. In its first year, the center served 165 families; 85 percent of the people who reserved space at the center had never canned before. As a hands-on kind of guy, Thompson was often at the center, coordinating the canning activities. With the center, the total amount of food being saved in Burlington skyrocketed. By 1975, more than 7,000 units of food were being processed at the center.

Other states caught wind of Burlington's community garden model, and, soon, people from across the United States were reaching out to Thompson and Gardens for All for guidance on how to create their own gardening networks. Thompson and a group of volunteers tried to keep up with the requests that poured in. Eventually, Gardens for All created a series of gardening books that were distributed to interested communities. The books contained advice on where to find land, how to get funding and where to find other community support. Thompson himself conducted gardening seminars in places like San Francisco, Atlanta, Ann Arbor, Philadelphia and Albuquerque. Garden's for All's annual Gallup poll found that, from 1971 to 1974, the percentage of people in America who were growing their own food increased by 8 percent, or by 8 million people. In 1974, roughly 33 million people had some type of vegetable garden, either in a community garden or at home.

For his efforts, Tommy received the Outdoor Recreation Achievement Award from the United States Department of the Interior. Like seeds in the wind, Tommy's community gardening idea continued to spread, landing all the way across the Atlantic. In November 1976, Tommy spoke at the International Leisure Gardening Congress in England, where people had begun looking for ways to make community garden sites permanent.

A garden plot in the Tommy Thompson Community Gardens. *Photograph courtesy of Thea Lewis.*

They discovered that, as the local gardening trend expanded, people took even more pride in their plots, and with continued oversight, there was less vandalism. In the United Kingdom and the United States, community gardens truly did create "community" and brought people together from all walks of life.

In *a Burlington Free Press* column called "Vermont Perspective," Thompson wrote:

> *Community gardens still epitomize the "melting pot" that serves all creeds and races. Poor and rich, illiterate and educated. People working with refugee groups in coastal cities learn that offering garden space is one of the best programs possible. The common subject of planting seeds and growing food seems to put people on equal footing right away.*

B.H. "Tommy" Thompson, the godfather of community gardening, died unexpectedly on March 22, 1983, of cardiac arrest. He was sixty-five years old. The man who inspired Vermonters and others to garden now has a garden of his own; the Tommy Thompson garden can be found at 282 Intervale Road in Burlington.

26.

MINNIE BLONDIN

DREAMS COME TRUE

Minnie Ella Breiner Blondin was born on January 14, 1915, to Charles and Zoe (Blair) Breiner. She was the first of fourteen children, and her family nicknamed her "Peanut," because, for years while she was growing up, she was still short enough to stand under the kitchen table without hitting her head. On June 6, 1936, she married Clifford M. Blondin in the Cathedral of the Immaculate Conception in downtown Burlington, a Catholic church that was lost to a fire during a spate of arsons in the 1970s. The pair had three sons: Charles, Robert and Arthur.

The busy mother of three growing boys became synonymous with one of Burlington's greatest organizations for children and families, the Sara Holbrook Community Center. The Center was the brainchild of Sara M. Holbrook, a psychologist and professor at the University of Vermont. Holbrook had worked in the settlement houses of New York City, where members of the community could receive healthcare and other services, increase their employment opportunities and find recreation. The settlement house movement, a boon to American immigrants, began in 1800s London, as the well-to-do students of Oxford and Cambridge began living and working with the poor to help them improve their quality of life.

With Dr. Bertha Terrill, a chairman of the home economics department at UVM, and a group of like-minded community members, Holbrook secured funding to bring her own settlement house to Burlington. She opened her first location in November 1937, in the storefront of an old pool hall at 116 Cherry Street. Minnie Blondin was the director. The center was well received by the low-income families of the area, many of whom had suffered generational poverty, and by other, more middle-class families, too. It quickly became a refuge that fostered a sense of community and cooperation. Social agencies, like the Burlington Boys and Girls Club and the Committee on Temporary Shelter (COTS), grew from her plan. The center was a bustling place, and it housed a multi-generational community. There, Irish, French-Canadian and Italian immigrants could study for citizenship tests and take classes in cooking and sewing. They could bring their children and grandchildren along, as well, to play in the free nursery school. There were dance classes and scout meetings at the center, and it offered well-child clinics with immunizations

Wherever she was, Minnie's mind was on improving the lives of children and families. She once recalled walking through Battery Park on her way to the center, and she saw children with their feet in dangling in a fountain. It occurred to her that the park could use a playground, so she went to propose the idea to one of the park's supervisors. The result was a shaded space with generous sandboxes, high-flying swings and a long slide that attracted children from all over the neighborhood. Sometimes, kids were so excited to visit the new park that they would arrive half-dressed, and adults would have to send them home to finish the job. Minnie eventually became one of the park's supervisors. Her events were inventive and infectious. Her pet shows and doll shows drew hundreds, and one of the latter was even featured in *LIFE Magazine*.

Minnie also drew people in with the center's dance recitals. She wanted kids to be able to show their proud parents, grandparents, aunts and uncles what they'd learned in the center's dance classes. The author of this book's earliest memory of Minnie Blondin was from a Sara Holbrook Center dance recital that she participated in when she was just four years old. Her mother, Claire Gestner, recounts:

> *At the time, we lived with her grandmother and great-grandfather in Burlington's Old North End. Her grandmother, my mother, was a seamstress at a sewing factory in Winooski. Money was tight, and recreational opportunities were slim. We enrolled her in tap classes, and she couldn't wait to perform. At the recital, she was the youngest in the chorus line. She shuffle-hop-stepped away in a top hat and sparkly tails that were made by her grandmother, belting out the lyrics to the song "Bushel and a Peck." She was so little but eager to please, and Minnie*

taught responsibility by example, so she knew she was to do her best. Minnie also expected the older girls, who were lined up on stage, to keep the little ones focused and out of mischief.

On another occasion, my daughter had a memorable interaction with Minnie that embarrasses her to this day, even though it happened nearly six decades ago. The annual Christmas parties at the center were a big deal to the community. There was always a crush of kids, parents and volunteers and a happy, confusing buzz, but Minnie maintained her composure and cheer in the face of the chaos; no one was sure how, but she did. When my daughter was four, she had finally developed a keen interest in Santa and couldn't wait to see what he would give her at the party.

When he arrived, the kids excitedly lined up so he could give everyone their presents and a candy cane (a bigger deal to kids in 1962 than it is these days). Do you know the expression, "You get what you get, and you don't get upset?" Well, I should have mentioned it to my daughter before she sat on St. Nickolas's lap. He handed her a gift, and she ran off with it and the candy cane, headed in the direction of her grandmother so that she could show it off. She unwrapped the present with lightning speed and discovered it was a box of crayons, something she had buckets of at home. She stomped her tiny, Mary Jane–wearing feet a few times, threw her head back and howled like a banshee before dissolving into hysterical sobs. Then, in a final, dramatic touch, she threw her peppermint candy cane on the floor, shattering it. We were mortified as Minnie came hurrying over to check on the ruckus. She held my child in her arms and asked what the issue was. Minnie listened, and she looked at the dwindling pile of gifts across the room and asked my daughter what she had wanted. Seeing a dark-haired little boy directly across from us, who was maybe seven or eight years old, gratefully unwrapping a colorful four-pack of Play-Doh, my kid pointed her chubby finger and hiccuped, "That," before wailing again. I'm not sure how she did it, but Minnie actually talked the poor kid into trading. But, then, that was Minnie—always a problem solver.

Whatever the center's location, when Minnie was in charge, the children who were headed there to play, take lessons or attend scout meetings simply told their parents they were "going to Minnie's." Their mothers and fathers knew exactly what they meant, and they trusted that their children would be in good hands, because they had gone to Minnie's when they were young. (She was never called, "Mrs. Blondin," only "Minnie"; it didn't matter if you were the mayor, a newspaper reporter, a parent or the tiniest child.)

Minnie had numerous honors bestowed upon her over the years. In 1968, she was made an honorary member of Vermont Alpha chapter of the Delta Kappa Gamma Society, an international organization of women in education, for being a "true friend, teacher and advisor" to people, both young and old. She was once quoted as saying, "I think I'm very fortunate. Not everyone gets to see their dream come true." Minnie held the position of director of the Sara M. Holbrook Center for thirty-four years before she retired in 1976. The center declared a "Minnie Blondin Day"; even after retirement, she was not forgotten. For years afterward, until she died, Minnie's mailbox was flooded each Christmas with more than one hundred cards sent by "her kids" from the center.

Minnie Blondin, director of the Sara Holbrook Community Center. *Photograph courtesy of the* Burlington Free Press.

Minnie died on August 16, 2012. She lived to be nearly one hundred years old. When asked the secret to her longevity, Minnie would often chuckle and say, "God doesn't want me, and the Devil isn't ready for me."

27

CHUCK AND JANN PERKINS

THE LAKEVIEW CHALET

Imagine: You're having lunch in the cemetery, when, suddenly, you spy through your car's windshield the intended inhabitants of one of your favorite mausoleums walking around outside the monument. What do you do? Do you go over and say hello? That's what the author of this book did the day she saw Chuck and Jann Perkins doing some weeding and general maintenance in the "yard" of their chalet-shaped final resting place at Lakeview on one sunny day in July.

Charles Norman Perkins Jr. was born in Burlington, Vermont. His wife, Janet Barbara (Couture) Perkins, was born in Springfield, Massachusetts. The two met while Jann was summering with her family on Malletts Bay in Colchester, Vermont. Chuck joked that she was the "girl next door" he only got to see two weeks out of the year. The couple married in Springfield, Massachusetts, in 1956.

In 1963, Chuck was working as a manager at the local JCPenney department store on Church Street in Burlington, when he and Jann, a graduate of the Holyoke Massachusetts School of Nursing, decided to buy a decrepit building on Williston Road in South Burlington, tear it down and turn it into a chalet-style building called the Alpine Shop, where they sold ski clothing and gear. The two figured they shared a love of the sport, so why not share it with others? They opened the store November 4, 1963, and their son, also named Chuck, was born three weeks later, truly making it a "family business"—especially after he learned to crawl.

Chuck and Jann Perkins. *Courtesy of the* VT Ski and Ride *magazine*.

Jann recalled how, one day, while she was working in the store, she heard someone exclaim, "What a cute baby!" She turned to see Chuck, who had made his way from the living quarters upstairs down to the sales floor. When his younger sister, Peg, came along, she also felt comfortable mingling with customers. Family lore says that she learned to ask, "May I help you?" before she could see over the counter.

The 1960s were ripe for Chuck and Jann's concept; 1966 was the year with the greatest number of ski areas in the state of Vermont—a total of eighty-one. The late 1060s and early 1970s saw the height of elite cross-country ski racing. In the late 1960s, International Business Machines (IBM) was even running advertisements in *SKIING Magazine*, in the hopes of recruiting young people looking for champagne powder to their Essex site. Bob Gray, a two-time Olympian who competed on the U.S. Nordic ski team from 1960 to 1974, lived and trained in Vermont. As did American cross-country skier and coach Martha Rockwell, who competed at the Winter Olympic Games in 1972 and 1976 and who had raced on the boys' team at the Putney School. In 1970, the Burke Mountain Academy

The Perkins monument. *Photograph courtesy of Thea Lewis.*

was founded as the first full-time U.S. ski academy; it was located in remodeled farmhouses on northeastern side of the mountain and gained a reputation as a high school that specialized in training ski racers.

Chuck and Jann expanded their business again and again, creating a place that became the state's largest alpine gear and clothing specialty retailers. Their store also became a legend in the Vermont ski industry. The couple hosted kick-offs for major brands, sponsored ski triathlons and debuted Warren Miller films, and they kept adding on to the business. They became avid fans of ski history and collectors of ski memorabilia; they even started a ski museum. In fact, it's hard to find something about Chuck and Jann that isn't related to skiing in some way.

Locals who have grown up with the Alpine Shop are delighted and amused to see the couple's little mausoleum, with its bronze doors on either side and clear glass "windows" with a view of the interior. The stained-glass medallions above both entrances depict an image of a man and woman skiing downhill. Flanking the doors are a pair of life-size granite skis engraved with their names, "Chuck" and "Jann."

There are Perkinses buried all around the chalet, including Chuck's Dad, Chuck Sr., who was a local doctor and City alderman with a great interest in Lake Champlain, and his mom, Florence, who passed away in 2004. Florence was written up in the *Burlington Free Press* in March 2003 for being Vermont's oldest citizen, at the age of 108 years and 8 months. Chuck attributed his mom's long life to her healthy habits and low-stress lifestyle. Jann said, "She never drank, never smoked and never swore." Chuck and Jann Perkins erected their ski chalet in Lakeview Cemetery in 2005. At the time of this writing, they are both very much alive.

BIBLIOGRAPHY

American Battlefield Trust. "Civil War Biography, Philip Sheridan." www. battlefields.org.

askART. "Charles Louis Heyde." www.askart.com.

Beachy, Jonathan. "10 Greatest Nurses of World War I." www.toprntobsn. com.

Burlington Board of Trade. "Brunswick, Maine as a Manufacturing, Business, and Commercial Center; with Brief Sketches of its History, Attractions, Leading Industries, and Institutions." rarebooksclub.com

Burlington Free Press. "A Card, Advertisement." June 7, 1869.

———. "A Hero Laid to Rest, Gen. Geo. Stannard." June 7, 1886.

———. "Announcement of City Ordinances." August 31, 1869.

———. "Burlington Traction Company to Pass to Other Hands." June 1, 1926

———. "City and Vicinity, Socrates Beach." March 30, 1893.

———. "Death Announcement, Gen. Oliver Otis Howard." October 27, 1909.

———. "Delta Kappa Gamma Society Initiates Minnie Blondin." May 8, 1968.

———. "Elias Lyman and Early Vermont." August 15, 1925.

———. "Elias Lyman Dies in His 74th Year." April 2, 1923.

———. "Fatal and Bloody Affray on Water Street." October 26, 1871.

———. "Funeral Announcement, Alvaro Adsit." March 30, 1923.

———. "Funeral of Judge Mower Largely Attended." April 29, 1940.

———. "Heirs Claim that Trustee of Socrates Beach Estate is too Parsimonious." February 18, 1926.

———. "Heyde's Paintings." July 3, 1867.

———. "History Space, Legacy of WWI at Lakeview Cemetery." October 14, 2018. www.loc.gov.

———. "Horatio Nelson Jackson, Book PBS Documentary Celebrate Trip." July 20, 2003.

———. "John J. Flynn Funeral" September 14, 1940.

———. "John J. Flynn, Dead at 86." September 13, 1940.

———. "Judge E.C. Mower Dies at 71. Lawyer, Educator and Banker." April 29, 1940.

———. "Laid to Rest: Funeral of General William Wells Largely Attended." May 4, 1892.

———. "Lawrence Barnes, A Sketch of His Life and Business Enterprises." June 22, 1886.

———. "Lieut. Col. Jackson To Head Regiment." January 16, 1922.

———. "Luella Wheeler Community Notes." N.d.

———. "MARRIED, Socrates Beach to Miss Abigail Hatch." January 16, 1850.

———. "Mayo Funeral Planned." May 27, 1937.

———. "Memorial to Miss Wheeler." June 2, 1919.

———. "Navy, Army and City of Burlington Pay Final Homage to Mayo." May 27, 1937.

———. "Obituary, Alvaro Adsit." March 28, 1923.

———. "Obituary, B.H. 'Tommy' Thompson." March 24, 1983.

———. "Obituary, Elihu Taft." January 14, 1929.

———. "Obituary, Hannah Louisa Howard." March 24, 1886.

———. "Obituary, H.O. Wheeler." July 18, 1918.

———. "Obituary, John Lyons." March 18, 1941.

———. "Obituary, John Purple Howard." October 29, 1885.

———. "Obituary, Leander Freeman." August 21, 1917.

———. "Obituary, Lettie Tracy." December 4, 1940.

———. "Obituary, Minnie Blondin." www.legacy.com.

———. "Obituary, Mrs. John J. Flynn, (Nellie)." December 11, 1922.

———. "Party to Honor Minnie Blondin." January 16, 2005.

———. "Perkinses Keep the Alpine Shop All in the Family." December 9, 1991.

———. "Philomene Lemoine Pasha Arrested." December 9, 1879.

———. "Philomene Lemoine vs. State of Vermont." January 8, 1881.

———. "Raid on Houses of Ill-Fame." August 1, 1877.

———. "Rain Doesn't Faze Minnie on Her Day." June 21, 1976.

———. "Shocking Homicide on Water Street." October 27, 1871.

———. "Star Drunkard Gets Long Sentence." September 16, 1910.

———. "Superintendent H.O. Wheeler Dies." July 17, 1918.

———. "Three Cheers for Beach!" October 17, 1862.

———. "Tommy Thompson, Gardens for All Founder Dies." March 24, 1983.

———. "Urban Woodbury Laid to Rest." April 19, 1915.

———. "WWI Veterans Buried at Lakeview Cemetery." October 15, 2018. www.burlingtonfreepress.com.

Burlington Journal. "Homeless Cite '27 Will in Demanding a Haven." September 1, 1989

Burns, Ken. *Horatio's Drive*. Aired in 2003 on PBS.

Bushnell, Mark. "Then Again: Speeding cross-country…at 20 mph." People and Places. www.vtdigger.org.

———. "Then Again: What the bishop Saw…" People and Places. November 11, 2018. www.vtdigger.org.

Cemeteries, Keith Eggener, December 13, 2010, W.W. Norton Company

Champlain College. "History of Perry Hall." www.champlain.edu.

Child, Hamilton. *Gazetteer and Business Directory of Chittenden County, Vermont, for 1882–83*. Cambridge, MA: Harvard University Journal Office, 1882.

Converse Home. "Home." www.conversehome.com.

Cross, David. "A Tale of Two Statues: The William Wells Statues at Gettysburg and Burlington." Vermont Historical Society (Winter/Spring 2005). www.vermonthistory.org.

Encyclopedia Britannica. "Oliver Otis Howard, United States Military Officer." www.britannica.com.

Find A Grave. "Socrates Beach." www.findagrave.com.

———. "Stillman Morgan Atherton Gillette." www.findagrave.com.

General Stannard House Committee. "Stannard's Story." General Stannard House. www.generalstannardhouse.org.

Graveline, Rose Mary. "John Ralph Lyons (188–1941)." BlackPast. www.blackpast.org.

Greenfield, Rebecca. "Our First Public Parks: The Forgotten History of Cemeteries." *Atlantic*, March 16, 2011.

Gresham, Tom. "Board Silly." First Published in *Business People* [Vermont], 2004. www.vermontguides.com.

Griffith, Roger M., and Lymnan Wood. *What a Way to Live and Make a Living: The Lyman P. Wood Story*. Tumwater, WA: Capitol City Press, 1994.

Hamblett, Barbara Knapp. "Cloud and Sunshine, Time and Season: UVM's Fleming Museum Celebrates the Vermont Landscapes of Charles Louis Heyde." *Vermont Quarterly* (Winter 2000). www.uvm.edu.

History. "Battle of Gettysburg: Union General George Stannard and the Second Vermont Brigade." History.com

Journal [Syracuse, NY]. Multiple articles.

Lewis, Thea. *Ghosts and Legends of Lake Champlain: The Bishop's Tale*. Charleston, SC: The History Press, August 21, 2012.

Lostflights.com. "January 16, 1942: Transcontinental & Western Air (TWA), Douglas DC-3 (NC1946) Potosi Mountain, NV." www.lostflights.com.

Margaret Lockwood Society. "Interview with Robert Matzen, Author of Fireball, Carole Lombard and the Mystery of Flight 3." www.margaretlockwoodsociety.wordpress.com.

Matzen, Robert. *Fireball: Carole Lombard and the Mystery of Flight 3*. Pittsburgh: GoodKnight Books, 2017.

New York Public Library. *Alvaro Adsit*. www.photographydatabase.org.

New York Times. "Retired Vermont Educator Was Advocate of Judicial Reform." April 26, 1940.

Norman Rockwell Museum of Vermont. "The Story of The Babysitter." www.facebook.com/NRMVT.

Oliver Otis Howard Papers. George J. Mitchell Department of Special Collections and Archives. Bowdoin College Library, Brunswick, Maine.

PBS. "American Nurses in WWI." www.pbs.org.

———. "New Perspectives on the West, Oliver Otis Howard." www.pbs.org.

People and Places. John J. Flynn. www.sites.google.com.

Polston, Pamela. "Heyde Seek." *Seven Days*, January 24, 2001.

———. "UVM Repurposes Former Taft School as Arts Center." *Seven Days*, November 7, 2018.

Robert Hull Fleming Museum. "Old Summits, Far-Surrounding Vales: The Vermont Landscape Paintings of Charles Louis Heyde (1822–1892), January 2001." www.tfaoi.com.

Thibault, Amanda. *This Place in History*. "General William Wells." Aired October 2016, on WPTZ. www.mychamplainvalley.com.

Thomas Duke. "'The Story of Harry Tracy, Super-Outlaw' Celebrated Criminal Cases of America, Part II: Pacific Coast Cases." www.historicalcrimedetective.com.

Thompson's Point. "Monk Cottage, 1910." www.thompsonspoint.org.

University Green Area Heritage Study. "Elihu B. Taft School, 404 Pearl Street." www.uvm.edu.

Vermont Community Garden Network. "A History of Community Gardening in Chittenden County, Vermont." www.vcgn.org.

Vermont Secretary of State (Office). "Governor Urban Woodbury, Farewell Address." www.sec.state.vt.us.

Walsh, Molly. "Value of Rockwell Painting Re-Examined in Vermont Burlington Free Press." *USA Today*, December 15, 2013.

Walt Whitman Archive. "Home" www.whitmanarchive.org.

Wikipedia. "General William Wells." www.wikipedia.org.

———. "Harry Tracy." www.wikipedia.org.

———. "Urban A. Woodbury." www.wikipedia.org.

Women's Memorial. "World War I Nurses: The Journal of Emma Elizabeth Weaver." www.womensmemorial.org.

Wood, Nancy. "Commentary: The Charlotte Way of Doing Business." *Charlotte News*, September 24, 2015. www.charlottenewsvt.org.

ABOUT THE AUTHOR

T hea Lewis is a Vermont native and the creator of Queen City Ghostwalk, the haunted tour chosen as the "Best Scary Stroll" by *Yankee Magazine*. Called Vermont's *Queen of Halloween*, Lewis has been scaring up history in Burlington and beyond since 2002, with her tours, special events and books she writes for adults and children. This is her fifth book with The History Press. Her other titles include *Haunted Burlington: Spirits of Vermont's Queen City*, *Ghosts and Legends of Lake Champlain*, *Haunted Inns and Ghostly Getaways of Vermont* and *Wicked Vermont*. In addition to her work with The History Press, Thea has also written a children's book, *There's A Witch in My Sock Drawer!* (Peapod Press, 2011).

You can find Thea online at queencityghostwalk.com, thealewis.com and on Facebook.